The Cyclist's
TRAINING DIARY

INTRODUCTION BY
JOE FRIEL

BOULDER, COLORADO

3002 Sterling Circle, Suite 100
Boulder, Colorado 80301-2338 USA
(303) 440-0601 · Fax (303) 444-6788 · E-mail velopress@competitorgroup.com

For information on purchasing VeloPress books, please call (800) 811-4210, ext. 2138, or visit www.velopress.com.

Distributed in the United States and Canada by Ingram Publisher Services

Front cover photo by Casey B. Gibson; back and inside cover photos and photo on page 25
  by Graham Watson
Cover design by Anita Koury
Interior design by Elizabeth Watson

Library of Congress Cataloging-in-Publication Data
Friel, Joe.
  The cyclist's training diary / by Joe Friel.
    p. cm.
  Includes bibliographical references.
    ISBN-13: 978-1-934030-08-0 (pbk.: alk. paper)
  1. Cycling—Training—Charts, diagrams, etc. 2. Bicycle racing—Training—Charts, diagrams, etc. I. Title.
  GV1048.F754 2007
  796.6—dc22

                                                    2007019878

13 / 10 9 8

CONTENTS

Introduction by Joe Friel

Any coach will tell you that a carefully maintained training record is a great tool for faster, stronger racing. Some cyclists are good at keeping a training diary, but others fail to take the time. Without a diary you're forced to rely on memory, which, all too often, provides only exaggerated versions of what happened months, weeks, or even days before.

There are several other good reasons to keep a diary. It can serve as a positive reinforcement and boost confidence before particularly challenging races. By looking back to workouts or other races that loomed large, but were mastered, you feel assured that you have what it takes. A diary also reveals whether or not fitness is improving by comparing recent measures such as time trials, interval results, or even resting heart rates against similar standards a year or more ago when you were in great shape. In the same way, you can thumb back through a diary to discover what has and hasn't worked before. This could be a peaking procedure prior to an especially good race, a way of dealing with an injury that once proved successful, or a tactic that worked against a strong competitor.

Perhaps the main argument for using a diary is in the prevention of overtraining—a necessity for nearly every serious athlete. More on this later.

WHAT IS A TRAINING DIARY?

Record-keeping works best in accomplishing the above if it's in the form of both a daily log and journal. Technically, a log is a record of basic data, usually numbers, that relate to progress (distance, time, heart rate, etc.), while a journal is a record of your thoughts and experiences. Log information is objective while the journal portion is subjective.

Both are important. By combining the two into a diary, the information you collect covers a broader spectrum of needs. You may decide not to use all the spaces provided in this diary—that's okay.

Whatever you write down, make it only what's important and useful to you. Everything else just gets in the way when trying to analyze your training.

THE "O" WORD

The diary is most commonly used to avoid overtraining. When it seems that training isn't going well, and you aren't quite sure why, looking back through diary notes for the last few weeks may reveal a cause of the problem. Look for phrases used repeatedly such as "feel tired" or "no snap today" or "sluggish." These are sure signs that you're doing too much—overreaching. Also check the numbers for trends and patterns.

You may find that every third day or so sleep quality is poor and fatigue is high. Such a pattern is telling you to allow more recovery time between the hard workouts. Another possible sign of doing too much is when heart rate data and workout ratings don't agree. For example, your heart rate is low, but the effort seems high. Such a review of the training diary helps you decide if it's time to take a long break or to just cut back for a couple of days.

JUST SAY "NO" TO COMPULSION

Keeping a diary is helpful for making progress in cycling, but don't let it become a handicap to your training and racing. Riders who believe they must achieve and record certain numbers in their training diary each week often lose focus of what riding a bike is all about—having fun! This diary is merely a tool to help you achieve your cycling goals, and a record of what you accomplish this year. Using a training diary as described here won't guarantee your success as a cyclist. It will, however, increase the likelihood. Happy riding!

HOW TO PLAN YOUR SEASON

Cyclists are goal-driven people. Show me a rider who has no desire to ride stronger and faster, and I'll show you a rider who is not in the sport for long. Success is not possible in cycling without high motivation. Racing a bike is just too grueling to do in an indifferent manner. Every cyclist wants to improve, but a passion to excel is nothing without a passion to prepare to excel.

Preparation is where many cyclists fail. Most are willing to put in endless hours on the road or trail, but are less zealous when it comes to planning. That's a shame, because planning is the first step in achieving any goal in life, including those accomplished on a bike. A goal without a plan is just a wish.

Most cyclists could achieve their goals by making only one small change: writing down a plan for how to train throughout the year. Just as with a diary, training plans may comprise the most minute particulars or provide just a rough outline. Regardless of the detail, better racing will result from deciding in advance what you'll do on the bike and when.

The Annual Training Plan (see page 19) is a tool that will help you incorporate periodization into your training. Periodization is a way of training in which fitness is built from the most basic to the more complex aspects in stages or periods. The purpose of periodization is fast racing when it counts.

The following step-by-step description guides you through each part of the Annual Training Plan that follows. It may take you thirty minutes or so to design your personal plan—time well invested. It's best to write only in pencil as things are likely to change during the season.

STEP 1: SET YOUR SEASON GOALS

What are three major racing accomplishments you'd like to achieve this year? Write them down on the plan. Keep it to three or less as having more is likely to complicate your training and racing. Goals are best if they're realistic, specific, measurable, and performance-oriented. Here is an example of a goal that meets these criteria:

Break one hour for the 40 km individual time trial by August 1.

Goals are most effective when they're written down and reviewed frequently. You can also write your goals on the jacket flap so that you'll see them every time you open your training diary.

STEP 2: IDENTIFY YOUR TRAINING OBJECTIVES

Training objectives are the aspects of fitness or the workout performances needed to achieve your season goals. Just as with the goals, objectives are best if realistic, specific, measurable, and performance-oriented. You can also write these objectives on the diary flap so you'll see them often. An example of a training objective that might support the above example of a season goal is:

*Complete 3 x 10 km intervals at 25 mph average with
5-minute recoveries by July 12.*

STEP 3: ESTABLISH YOUR ANNUAL HOURS

How many hours did you train last year? Are you capable of riding your bike more, or do you need to cut back this year due to time constraints? Would you like to race more competitively this year, or is this a year just to maintain your race level? The answers to these questions will help you decide how many hours to train in the coming year. There is a relationship between how many hours or miles you ride in a year and how you race. If you're unsure of your hours from last year due to poor record-keeping, now is a good time to start rectifying that problem.

Here are suggested annual hours by sport and racer category. These are not absolutes; in other words, you don't have to train at these hours to race in these categories. Some riders do more and still race poorly. Others do less and win frequently.

Road Category	Annual Hours
Pro	800–1200
1–2	700–1000
3/35+ Masters	500–700
4/45+ Masters	350–500
5/Juniors	200–350

Mountain Bike Category	Annual Hours
Pro	700–1000
Semi-Pro	600–800
Expert/Veteran	500–700
Sport/Master	300–500
Beginner/Junior	200–350

STEP 4: FILL IN THE CALENDAR

In the column titled "Week/Mon." write in the dates of each Monday in the year. For example, January 5 is 1/5.

STEP 5: PLAN YOUR YEAR OF RACING

List all of the races you may do this year in the "Races" column, placing them in the proper weeks according to their dates. If unsure about a particular race, list it.

STEP 6: PRIORITIZE YOUR RACES

Give a priority ranking (in the column labeled "Pri.") to each of the races using the following guidelines:

A-Priority Races. These are the most important races—the ones that will determine success in the coming season. They are closely related to the Season Goals on the previous page. You will peak and taper for each of these races. Limit these to no more than four A races in a year. Two in the same week or a stage race counts as one A race. It's a good idea to "clump" two or more of these races together within a two- or three-week period. That way you can peak two or three times in a season. Trying to peak more times than this prevents you from coming into top form since there's not enough time between them to reestablish fitness.

B-Priority Races. These aren't as important as the A races, so you will not peak and taper for these races. A few days of rest, however, precede each event. Assign a B priority to about eight races, again counting two in the same week or a B-priority stage race as one.

C-Priority Races. These least important races are ones that you may not even do. You'll "train through them," meaning they are treated the same as a hard workout. They are best used as tune-up races before A- and B-priority races. They also make good workouts and build experience in novice riders. There are no limits on the number of C races, but they can interfere with training, so choose them conservatively. Frequent racing without a break is a common cause of burnout and overtraining.

STEP 7: IDENTIFY YOUR TRAINING PERIODS

This where the periodization begins. You now divide the season into periods starting with your A races. A clumping of A-priority races is called a "Race" period and may last as long as three weeks or as short as one. The week or two before each Race period, write in "Peak." Preceding each of these Peaks is a six- to nine-week "Build" period. The first Build period of the year is preceded by an eight- to twelve-week "Base" period and before that a two- to four-week "Prep" period. It's a good idea to plan for some rest after each of the Race periods by plugging in a one- to six-week "Transition."

The suggested characteristics of each of these periods are as follows:

Prep. General adaptation to training with weights, crosstraining, and on-bike drills. The emphasis is on endurance, force (weight room strength), and speed skills (pedaling and handling skills).

Base. Gradually increase the basic fitness elements of endurance, force, and speed skills. Begin muscular endurance with training near or just below lactate (anaerobic) threshold.

Build. Develop greater anaerobic endurance fitness with intervals and sprints while refining muscular endurance and power. Work especially on improving personal racing limiters and achieving Training Objectives. Maintain endurance, force, and speed skills. To maintain an ability all you need to do is complete the specific type of workout every 10 to 14 days or so.

Peak. Reduce volume and allow for more recovery days between hard workouts that simulate racing and refine needed skills. Do a mini-race simulation workout every 72 to 96 hours. This may be a group workout, hill repeats that simulate a climb in the race, sprints with a partner, or anything else that you believe is necessary for success in your upcoming A-priority race.

Race. A period of focused racing with greatly reduced training. Allow for lots of rest with frequent, short, race-intensity workouts.

Transition. An extended period of rest and recovery. This may be three to five days or as much as six weeks. It's okay to exercise during this break, but no "training."

You can use the blank fold-out annual calendar (pages 22a–22b) to keep track of what months your different training periods will fall in. This calendar is also useful to help you schedule testing and to decide what days of the week are best for particular workouts. Filling in the calendar will help you see your progression of weekly hours from month to month as well as your progression of races for the entire year. The calendar may also serve as a reminder to plan your training around events in your work or personal life.

STEP 8: FILL IN YOUR WEEKLY HOURS

Write in the approximate hours you will train each week, including weights and crosstraining, based on the Weekly Training Hours table (pages 22–23). The actual hours you work out each week will vary from this based on many circumstances such as weather or other unexpected complications. This is a guideline only. Feel free to change it to meet your exact needs.

STEP 9: TARGET YOUR MOST IMPORTANT WORKOUTS

Each week check the key workout types following the period guidelines offered above in Step 7. In the "Details" column you might list something such as "three-hour ride," "intervals," or "hills." Key workouts are described in the following terms. (For more details of each of these types of workouts, see *The Cyclist's Training Bible*.)

Weights. These are strength training workouts.

Endurance. These workouts emphasize the athlete's ability to delay the onset of fatigue and reduce its effects. This may include longer, low-intensity work.

Force. These workouts improve a cyclist's ability to overcome resistance. For example, biking on hills or in the wind.

Speed Skills. This training will help a cyclist move effectively on the bike. These workouts usually emphasize form and technique.

Muscular Endurance. These are workouts that train muscles to maintain a relatively high force load for a prolonged period of time, by combining force and endurance training.

Anaerobic Endurance. These workouts emphasize the cyclist's ability to resist fatigue at a very high level of effort with high leg turnover. This type of training may include long sprints or short climbs, and is best introduced later in the season.

Power. This training develops the cyclist's ability to apply maximum force quickly. This type of training usually involves short, all-out efforts, and is best done early in a training session before the body is fatigued.

Testing. Performed on recovery weeks, testing is a good way to measure your progress throughout a season.

HOW TO USE THIS DIARY

A training diary is only as useful as you make it. If you record little or write in it inconsistently, a diary has little value. On the other hand, recording lots of needless data that you never look at again not only wastes time, but also makes it harder to analyze later. The key is to write down immediately following every workout what was important and nothing more. The longer you wait, the greater the possibility you'll forget something or that feelings and thoughts will fade.

To ensure that it's used, keep this diary in a place that you go to following every ride, perhaps near where cycling shoes or workout gear is kept. That way you see it and are more likely to write in it right away. Your log is a constant reminder of your goals and progress. Filling it out after every workout will help to keep you on track throughout the season.

The text that follows describes the various parts of the diary pages that make up most of this book. You may decide not to use some parts, or you may want to modify the information you record in other parts from what is suggested here. The most important point is that you keep an accurate record of training and racing for future reference. The headings listed here can be found on each diary page.

WEEK BEGINNING

At the start of each week indicate Monday's date, and the dates for the other days of the week. These correspond with the "Week/Mon." column of the Annual Training Plan.

PERIOD

From the Annual Training Plan write in what training period this weeks falls into: Prep, Base, Build, Peak, Race, or Transition.

PLANNED HOURS

The approximate number of hours you plan to ride this week are recorded here based on what you wrote on the Annual Training Plan in the "Hours" column. This is a rough guideline only. You may decide to change this a little one way or the other. The idea, however, is to remain consistent with your plan so that a high-volume week remains much the same, as does a low-volume recovery week. On the other hand, if you aren't feeling right late in the week, it's better to cut back than to risk overtraining or illness. When in doubt—cut it out. Some riders prefer to record weekly volume in miles rather than hours. Record whichever works better for you.

WEEK GOALS

At the start of each week, write in three goals you want to accomplish that will help achieve your training objectives on the Annual Training Plan. For example, if one of your training objectives is to "Complete 3 x 10 km intervals at 25 mph average with 5-minute recoveries by July 12," then at some point in the season, after building the necessary fitness, this becomes a weekly goal. Prior to that, other weekly goals will build up to this with something such as: "Complete 3 x 8 km intervals at 25 mph average with 5-minute recoveries."

---

week beginning: _March 5_

Period: _Build 1_   **Planned Hours:** _15:00_

---

week goals: ✓ _Improve training consistency: Complete all BT workouts_
✓ _Improve climbing: Climb Rist Canyon in 28 minutes by 5/31_
✓ _Improve focus: Feel more focused in tempo workouts by 7/31_

MONDAY ___ / ___ / ___

Write in Monday's date (also write in dates for the other days of the week).

VITAL SIGNS (SLEEP, FATIGUE, STRESS, SORENESS)

The purpose of this part of the diary is to help you listen to your body. Every day it gives you clues about what condition it is in. By closely monitoring some of the signals it sends out, you can head off overtraining, burnout, injury, and illness. The first thing you should do every morning is rate your perceptions of the previous night's sleep, your fatigue level, psychological stress, and soreness. Use a scale of 1 to 7—with 1 being the best, most favorable rating, and 7 the worst, most unfavorable rating. Write the appropriate number in the box preceding each signal. A rating of 4 or greater on any of the vital signs above should be considered as warnings that something isn't right. The more warnings, the more cautiously and conservatively you should train on that day.

Resting heart rate should be taken while you are still in bed and recorded as beats per minute (bpm) above (+) or below (–) normal, based on a one-week average found when you were well rested. While a low pulse is usually a good sign for fitness, it is not always so. Some scientific studies have found obviously overtrained athletes to have low resting heart rates.

Also record your body weight right after getting out of bed. Fluctuations in weight could indicate that your diet is out of harmony with your needs. It could also be low hydration levels, emotional stress, and high training workloads. Consider a two-pound change in two days as a sign that something is wrong.

MONDAY _3_ / _17_ / _07_
_2_ sleep _3_ fatigue _1_ stress _2_ soreness
resting heart rate _+4_ weight _150_

PLANNED WORKOUT

At the start of the week, briefly summarize what you'll do in training each day and the intended duration of the workout. This will only take five to ten minutes and is time well spent when you consider how much time is put into daily training. The column on your Annual Training Plan called "Most Important Workouts" will help with this task. Schedule the general type of workout, such as endurance, intervals or hills, or write in a specific workout, such as:

4 x 10 minutes in zone 4 (3-minute recoveries)

You may even develop a code for specific workouts and record these in the back of the diary under "Notes" (see page 256). For even easier access, write these codes on the inside of the diary's jacket flap. In this part, also write in the planned duration of the workout in time or miles. These daily duration totals should approximately equal the weekly "Planned Hours/Miles" recorded at the top of the first page.

WEATHER, ROUTE, DISTANCE, TIME

As soon as you get off the bike, write in the details of the ride. This may include the major aspects of the weather like temperature, wind, snow, or rain. Later you may discover a pattern of weather-related problems, such as fading near the end of hot rides. It's also good to know when reviewing your log a year or more later what the conditions of the

weather _65 degrees with clouds_
route _Neva Loop_
distance _22 miles_ time _55:20_

workout were. This may explain why you were so fast or so slow on a given day. Also describe the route. Most cyclists have common routes with short names. You may want to note these in the Routes and Best Times section in the back of the diary (page 254). Write in the number of actual miles covered in the ride and the time, either elapsed workout time or time of day.

TIME BY ZONE

Summarize the heart rate intensity of the ride in these boxes by indicating how many minutes were spent in each zone. If your monitor has memory, you can easily indicate three zones ("above," "in," and "below" in heart rate monitor language). This is important information that will indicate if you're getting enough low-intensity riding early in the season, and if the weekly volume in the higher zones is adequate later in the season when a race period approaches. When you fill out this section following a race, it will give you better insight as to the intensities necessary to race and thus to train.

AVERAGE HEART RATE AND POWER

Average heart rate (Avg. HR) and average power (Avg. Power) are good indicators of how intense your workout was. Also, by comparing the two you get an excellent indicator of how your fitness is progressing. Divide your average power by your average heart rate to get a sense of how hard you are working to produce a certain level of power. Over time, this number will increase as your fitness improves.

WORKOUT RATING

Use this section in any way you prefer. You could, for example, "grade" the workout in terms of accomplishment. Another use is to indicate how hard the workout seemed or how you felt.

Your workout rating may serve as an additional signal that something isn't going well if the perception of intensity doesn't agree with the heart rate data, or if you see a pattern of feeling poorly. Then again, this section may serve as an encouraging reminder that everything is going well.

> avg. HR _____142_____ avg. power _____163_____
> zone 1 _2_ 2 _10_ 3 _27_ 4 _10_ 5 _6_
> workout rating _____B-_____

NOTES

This is the journal part of the diary. Record comments about your workout such as who you rode with, how you felt, interval heart rates, soreness, noticeable improvements, results of self-tests, or outside factors such as workouts that left you tired. Later, as you go back over the diary trying to figure out why you raced so well at some point, these comments will give life to the workout details logged above. It's also a good idea to record any changes made to your bike in this part, such as moving the saddle or installing new pedals. A few days or weeks later some problem such as knee pain may appear—knowing what changes were made and when helps in the detective work. You can also note such changes on the Bike Measurement Charts near the back of the diary (pages 252–253).

NUTRITION

Other than quality workouts and rest, nothing has as great an impact on your training and race performance as what you eat and when you eat it. Use this space to record any number of nutrition details for the day such as calories consumed; carbohydrate, fat, and protein intake; supplements used; dietary changes; your nutrition "grade" for the day; or anything else you feel is important.

RACE 1 AND RACE 2

Summarize the important details of any races done this week including an evaluation of how you did, what needs work, or tactics and strategies used. After races, you should also fill out the Season Results page at the back of the diary (page 255). This will come in handy when seeking new sponsors, looking for a new team, or applying for upgrades. It's also a quick reference to see how you did last year in this same race. For the full details of any race, you can then turn to the appropriate day in your log.

WEEKLY SUMMARY

Summarize the week by totaling weekly "Bike Time" and "Bike Miles." There is also space to total time and mileage for the "Year to Date" (YTD). This will come in handy at the end of the season when you start planning for next year. Keeping it tallied weekly is easier than going back and adding it up later. "Strength Time" tracks time in the weight room. The blank rows are there for crosstraining activities such as cross-country skiing, running, or swimming. Write in which activity was done and the totals. Describe any "Soreness" encountered, no matter how slight, in case it recurs or gets worse. Knowing when it started may help determine a cause. In the "Notes" section summarize how the week went.

RACING

race 1 _Springerton Classic_

category _3_

distance _58 miles_ time _2:32_

result _5th_ upgrade pts. _3_

notes _Felt strong, stayed w/leaders_
until the end

race 2 _Stazio Crit_

category _3_

distance _26 miles_ time _1:00_

result _18th_ upgrade pts. _____

~~notes~~ _Practice cornering!_

WEEKLY SUMMARY

	weekly total	YTD
bike time	_7:45_	_65:00_
bike miles	_120_	_1,360_
strength time	_1:30_	_15:00_
yoga	_1:15_	_6:00_
total	_10:15_	_86:00_

soreness _Tight IT band (left)_

notes _Replaced chain and cables._

OTHER DIARY USES

A training diary is the best place to store all sorts of basic information about your training, equipment, race results, and other personal details. At some time in the future—next month, next year, or three years from now—something will come up that you need to remember. How did I do in this race last time? How much volume did I do in my best year? How was my last bike set up? How much intense riding did I do last spring? The pages at the back of this diary offer ample room to keep track of many details and customize them to fit your exact needs and interests. This section will provide the answers quickly. Here are some possibilities.

TESTING

Periodic fitness testing is a great way to know if your training is on track. You may have a gut feel that you are in better shape now than a few weeks ago, but without some hard evidence there's no way to be sure. In this section (see page 238) you can record the results of your tests for future reference. Having test results when you know you were in great shape serves as a standard to gauge the results of similar tests in the future.

TEST TYPE

There are two general categories of tests—field tests and lab tests. And within those two broad categories there are more-defined testing protocols. See *The Cyclist's Training Bible* for examples of field tests you may do, such as a Graded Exercise Test, Aerobic Time Trial, or 30-Minute Time Trial.

HEART RATE AND POWER AT ANAEROBIC THRESHOLD

Many of the tests you do can help you determine your anaerobic (lactate) threshold (AT). This is a critical physiological point that can be generally defined as the intensity level at which lactate accumulates in your bloodstream more quickly than it can be processed. The most common indicators used to identify your AT heart rate and power. Whenever a test identifies either of these landmarks, record it here.

ZONES

Once you know your AT you can set up training intensity zones for power and heart rate. Again, see *The Cyclist's Training Bible* for heart rate zones. For power, use these ranges:

Zone 1	less than 56% of AT power
Zone 2	56–75% of AT power
Zone 3	76–90% of AT power
Zone 4	91–100% of AT power
Zone 5a	101–105% of AT power
Zone 5b	106–120% of AT power
Zone 5c	more than 120% of AT power

VO₂MAX AND BODY FAT

If your test identifies these metrics, record them here for future reference.

NOTES

Make notes on details that have an effect on test results such as equipment used, pre-test meals, warm-up, and equipment calibration. Also record the precise protocol used in the test.

TRAINING GRIDS

Training and fitness trends are more easily seen when information is graphed. The blank grids provided here (see page 241) can be used to record the training data that are most important to you on a monthly and yearly basis. For example, you may choose to display weekly training hours or miles; the longest weekly ride; the volume of weekly high-intensity training (a good predictor of performance); or daily heart rates, either waking, recovery, or post-workout. You can probably come up with other creative ways to use this section.

Here's an idea that combines both the duration of a workout with its intensity and is easily graphed to reveal how hard you're actually training: Assign a "workload" value to a ride. One way of doing this is to multiply the number of minutes in a zone by the numeric name of the heart rate zone. For example, if you spent ten minutes in zone 4 on a given ride, the workload is 40 (10 x 4) for that portion of the ride. The total workload for a ride is the combined workloads for each of the five heart rate zones. While not a perfect system, this allows you to roughly determine what kind of stress is applied each day. Graphing cumulative workloads for a week on one of these grids rather than merely recording miles, gives you a better idea of how your training is going.

The following is an example of a daily cumulative workload graph for one month of workouts.

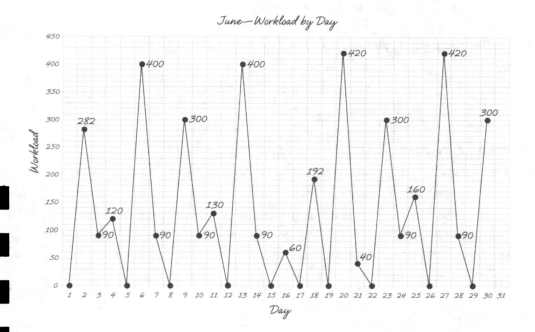

June—Workload by Day

BIKE MEASUREMENT CHARTS

Have you ever changed your saddle position and then tried to set it back to the original position only to find that it was never quite right again? Completing this diagram (see pages 252–253) with your exact measurements will resolve this once and for all. It will also allow you to set up a new bike to your exact position without a lot of trial and error. Any time equipment is adjusted, having a position record can potentially save lots of time and frustration.

ROUTES AND BEST TIMES

If you're like most cyclists, you have established routes that you frequently ride. Sometimes at the end of a workout you realize that you rode especially fast and try to remember what your previous times were on this same course. Here (page 254) is the place to note such times for later reference. Another use for this section is as a record of self-tests. For example, pick out a flat five-mile course and ride it at a given heart rate, say 9 to 11 beats below your lactate threshold heart rate, in a standard gear. If you've done a good job of controlling variables such as warm-up, rest, diet, and weather, decreasing times are a sign that fitness is improving. This is called an "aerobic time trial." Monthly, all-out time trials on a standard course also serve as good indicators of progress when done regularly, especially before the race season begins.

SEASON RESULTS

Keep a good record of your race results on the page provided at the back (page 255). This will come in handy when it's time to seek a sponsor, join a new team, apply for an upgrade, or just remember how you did last year.

RACE DAY CHECKLIST

Almost every rider forgets something critical on race day, like bike shoes or helmet, at least once a year. Your memory just isn't good enough sometimes to recall all of the many items needed. The night before a race, gather your gear together and check it off in pencil (see page 260). That reduces the race day stress the next morning and allows your mind to relax and think about riding well instead of wondering whether or not your sunglasses are packed.

NOTES

I've made every attempt to cover all aspects of training in this introduction, but some little tidbit of information is sure to come up. For example, what products and therapies seem to work for you when a cold starts coming on? If you only get one or two colds each year, it's hard to remember. Write it here (see page 256). How about the combination for your padlock at the health club? Ever forget that? Jot it down. You could also keep track of personal best lifts in the weight room, the phone numbers of riding partners, or any number of other details. Write down anything that will free your mind to focus on riding faster.

Whether you train with a coach or independently, there is much to be learned from a year of training if you know what to watch for. I hope that you will use this diary to improve your cycling and get even more enjoyment from the sport from year to year.

Joe Friel has trained endurance athletes since 1980. Joe has authored The Cyclist's Training Bible, Cycling Past 50, Total Heart Rate Training, The Triathlete's Training Bible, The Mountain Biker's Training Bible, Your First Triathlon, Going Long: Training for Ironman-Distance Triathlons (coauthor), *and* The Paleo Diet for Athletes (coauthor). *He holds a masters degree in exercise science and is a USA Triathlon– and USA Cycling–certified coach. His services are described in detail on his Web site www.trainingbible.com.*

annual training plan

SEASON GOALS

1. _____
_____
_____

2. _____
_____
_____

3. _____
_____
_____

TRAINING OBJECTIVES

1. _____
_____
_____

2. _____
_____
_____

3. _____
_____

4. _____
_____

5. _____
_____
_____

ANNUAL HOURS____

week / mon.	race	pri.	period	hours	details	workouts							
						WEIGHTS	ENDURANCE	FORCE	SPEED SKILL	MUSCULAR ENDURANCE	ANAEROBIC ENDURANCE	POWER	TESTING
01 /													
02 /													
03 /													
04 /													
05 /													
06 /													
07 /													
08 /													
09 /													
10 /													
11 /													
12 /													
13 /													
14 /													
15 /													
16 /													
17 /													
18 /													
19 /													
20 /													
21 /													
22 /													
23 /													
24 /													
25 /													
26 /													

Period: _____   **Planned Hours:** _____

MONDAY _____/_____/_____

■ sleep   ■ fatigue   ■ stress   ■ soreness

resting heart rate_____weight_____

planned workout_____

_____

_____

weather_____

route_____

_____

_____

dist._____time_____

zone 1_____2_____3_____4_____5_____

avg. HR_____avg. power_____

workout rating_____

notes _____

_____

_____

_____

_____

_____

_____

_____

_____

nutrition _____

_____

_____

_____

_____

TUESDAY_____/_____/_____

■ sleep   ■ fatigue   ■ stress   ■ soreness

resting heart rate_____weight_____

planned workout_____

_____

_____

weather_____

route_____

_____

_____

dist._____time_____

zone 1_____2_____3_____4_____5_____

avg. HR_____avg. power_____

workout rating_____

notes _____

_____

_____

_____

_____

_____

_____

_____

_____

nutrition _____

_____

_____

_____

_____

week goals: ■ _____
■ _____
■ _____

WEDNESDAY____/____/____

■ sleep ■ fatigue ■ stress ■ soreness

resting heart rate_____weight_____

planned workout_____
_____
_____

weather_____

route_____
_____
_____
_____

dist._____time_____

zone 1_____2_____3_____4_____5_____

avg. HR_____avg. power_____

workout rating_____

notes _____
_____
_____
_____
_____
_____
_____
_____
_____

nutrition _____
_____
_____
_____

THURSDAY____/____/____

■ sleep ■ fatigue ■ stress ■ soreness

resting heart rate_____weight_____

planned workout_____
_____
_____

weather_____

route_____
_____
_____
_____

dist._____time_____

zone 1_____2_____3_____4_____5_____

avg. HR_____avg. power_____

workout rating_____

notes _____
_____
_____
_____
_____
_____
_____
_____
_____

nutrition _____
_____
_____
_____

FRIDAY _____/_____/_____

- sleep - fatigue - stress - soreness

resting heart rate_____weight_____

planned workout_____

_____

_____

weather_____

route_____

_____

_____

_____

_____

dist._____time_____

zone 1_____2_____3_____4_____5_____

avg. HR_____avg. power_____

workout rating_____

notes _____

_____

_____

_____

_____

_____

_____

_____

_____

nutrition _____

_____

_____

_____

_____

SATURDAY_____/_____/_____

- sleep - fatigue - stress - soreness

resting heart rate_____weight_____

planned workout_____

_____

_____

weather_____

route_____

_____

_____

_____

_____

dist._____time_____

zone 1_____2_____3_____4_____5_____

avg. HR_____avg. power_____

workout rating_____

notes _____

_____

_____

_____

_____

_____

_____

_____

_____

nutrition _____

_____

_____

_____

_____

SUNDAY _____/_____/_____

☐ sleep ☐ fatigue ☐ stress ☐ soreness

resting heart rate_____weight_____

planned workout_____

_____

_____

weather_____

route_____

_____

_____

_____

_____

dist._____time_____

zone 1_____2_____3_____4_____5_____

avg. HR_____avg. power_____

workout rating_____

notes _____

_____

_____

_____

_____

_____

_____

_____

_____

_____

nutrition _____

_____

_____

_____

_____

_____

RACING

race 1 _____

category_____

distance_____time _____

result _____upgrade pts. _____

notes _____

_____

_____

_____

race 2 _____

category_____

distance_____time _____

result _____upgrade pts. _____

notes _____

_____

_____

WEEKLY SUMMARY

	weekly total	YTD
bike time		
bike miles		
strength time		
total		

soreness _____

notes _____

_____

_____

_____

_____

_____

Period: _____   **Planned Hours:** _____

MONDAY _____/_____/_____

☐ sleep ☐ fatigue ☐ stress ☐ soreness

resting heart rate_____weight_____

planned workout_____

_____

_____

weather_____

route_____

_____

_____

_____

dist._____time_____

zone 1_____2_____3_____4_____5_____

avg. HR_____avg. power_____

workout rating_____

notes _____

_____

_____

_____

_____

_____

_____

_____

_____

nutrition _____

_____

_____

_____

_____

TUESDAY _____/_____/_____

☐ sleep ☐ fatigue ☐ stress ☐ soreness

resting heart rate_____weight_____

planned workout_____

_____

_____

weather_____

route_____

_____

_____

_____

dist._____time_____

zone 1_____2_____3_____4_____5_____

avg. HR_____avg. power_____

workout rating_____

notes _____

_____

_____

_____

_____

_____

_____

_____

_____

nutrition _____

_____

_____

_____

_____

week goals: ∎ _____
∎ _____
∎ _____

WEDNESDAY___/___/___

▪ sleep ▪ fatigue ▪ stress ▪ soreness

resting heart rate_____weight_____

planned workout_____

_____

_____

weather_____

route_____

_____

_____

_____

dist._____time_____

zone 1_____2_____3_____4_____5_____

avg. HR_____avg. power_____

workout rating_____

notes _____

_____

_____

_____

_____

_____

_____

_____

_____

_____

_____

nutrition _____

_____

_____

_____

_____

THURSDAY___/___/___

▪ sleep ▪ fatigue ▪ stress ▪ soreness

resting heart rate_____weight_____

planned workout_____

_____

_____

weather_____

route_____

_____

_____

_____

dist._____time_____

zone 1_____2_____3_____4_____5_____

avg. HR_____avg. power_____

workout rating_____

notes _____

_____

_____

_____

_____

_____

_____

_____

_____

_____

_____

nutrition _____

_____

_____

_____

_____

FRIDAY _____/_____/_____

☐ sleep ☐ fatigue ☐ stress ☐ soreness

resting heart rate_____weight_____

planned workout_____

_____

_____

weather_____

route_____

_____

_____

_____

_____

dist._____time_____

zone 1_____2_____3_____4_____5_____

avg. HR_____avg. power_____

workout rating_____

notes _____

_____

_____

_____

_____

_____

_____

_____

_____

_____

_____

nutrition _____

_____

_____

_____

_____

SATURDAY_____/_____/_____

☐ sleep ☐ fatigue ☐ stress ☐ soreness

resting heart rate_____weight_____

planned workout_____

_____

_____

weather_____

route_____

_____

_____

_____

_____

dist._____time_____

zone 1_____2_____3_____4_____5_____

avg. HR_____avg. power_____

workout rating_____

notes _____

_____

_____

_____

_____

_____

_____

_____

_____

_____

_____

nutrition _____

_____

_____

_____

_____

SUNDAY _____/_____/_____

☐ sleep ☐ fatigue ☐ stress ☐ soreness

resting heart rate_____weight_____

planned workout_____

_____

_____

weather_____

route_____

_____

_____

_____

_____

dist._____time_____

zone 1_____2_____3_____4_____5_____

avg. HR_____avg. power_____

workout rating_____

notes _____

_____

_____

_____

_____

_____

_____

_____

_____

_____

_____

_____

nutrition _____

_____

_____

_____

_____

RACING

race 1 _____

category_____

distance_____time _____

result _____upgrade pts. _____

notes _____

_____

_____

_____

race 2 _____

category_____

distance_____time _____

result _____upgrade pts. _____

notes _____

_____

_____

WEEKLY SUMMARY

	weekly total	YTD
bike time		
bike miles		
strength time		
total		

soreness _____

notes _____

_____

_____

_____

_____

_____

_____

Period: _____ **Planned Hours:** _____

MONDAY _____/_____/_____

■ sleep ■ fatigue ■ stress ■ soreness

resting heart rate_____weight_____

planned workout_____

_____

_____

weather_____

route_____

_____

_____

dist._____time_____

zone 1_____2_____3_____4_____5_____

avg. HR_____avg. power_____

workout rating_____

notes _____

_____

_____

_____

_____

_____

_____

_____

nutrition _____

_____

_____

_____

_____

TUESDAY_____/_____/_____

■ sleep ■ fatigue ■ stress ■ soreness

resting heart rate_____weight_____

planned workout_____

_____

_____

weather_____

route_____

_____

_____

dist._____time_____

zone 1_____2_____3_____4_____5_____

avg. HR_____avg. power_____

workout rating_____

notes _____

_____

_____

_____

_____

_____

_____

_____

nutrition _____

_____

_____

_____

week goals: ■ _____

■ _____

■ _____

WEDNESDAY ____/____/____

■ sleep ■ fatigue ■ stress ■ soreness

resting heart rate_____weight_____

planned workout_____

_____

_____

weather_____

route_____

_____

_____

dist._____time_____

zone 1_____2_____3_____4_____5_____

avg. HR_____avg. power_____

workout rating_____

notes _____
_____
_____
_____
_____
_____
_____

nutrition _____
_____
_____
_____

THURSDAY ____/____/____

■ sleep ■ fatigue ■ stress ■ soreness

resting heart rate_____weight_____

planned workout_____

_____

_____

weather_____

route_____

_____

_____

dist._____time_____

zone 1_____2_____3_____4_____5_____

avg. HR_____avg. power_____

workout rating_____

notes _____
_____
_____
_____
_____
_____
_____

nutrition _____
_____
_____
_____

FRIDAY _____/_____/_____

◼ sleep ◼ fatigue ◼ stress ◼ soreness

resting heart rate_____weight_____

planned workout_____

_____

_____

weather_____

route_____

_____

_____

_____

_____

dist._____time_____

zone 1_____2_____3_____4_____5_____

avg. HR_____avg. power_____

workout rating_____

notes _____

_____

_____

_____

_____

_____

_____

_____

_____

_____

nutrition _____

_____

_____

_____

SATURDAY_____/_____/_____

◼ sleep ◼ fatigue ◼ stress ◼ soreness

resting heart rate_____weight_____

planned workout_____

_____

_____

weather_____

route_____

_____

_____

_____

_____

dist._____time_____

zone 1_____2_____3_____4_____5_____

avg. HR_____avg. power_____

workout rating_____

notes _____

_____

_____

_____

_____

_____

_____

_____

_____

nutrition _____

_____

_____

_____

SUNDAY ____/____/____

■ sleep ■ fatigue ■ stress ■ soreness

resting heart rate_____weight_____

planned workout_____

_____

_____

weather_____

route_____

_____

_____

_____

_____

dist._____time_____

zone 1_____2_____3_____4_____5_____

avg. HR_____avg. power_____

workout rating_____

notes _____

_____

_____

_____

_____

_____

_____

_____

_____

_____

nutrition _____

_____

_____

_____

RACING

race 1 _____

category_____

distance_____time _____

result _____upgrade pts. _____

notes _____

_____

_____

_____

race 2 _____

category_____

distance_____time _____

result _____upgrade pts. _____

notes _____

_____

_____

WEEKLY SUMMARY

	weekly total	YTD
bike time		
bike miles		
strength time		
total		

soreness _____

notes _____

_____

_____

_____

_____

_____

_____

Period: _____   **Planned Hours:** _____

MONDAY _____/_____/_____

☐ sleep ☐ fatigue ☐ stress ☐ soreness

resting heart rate_____weight_____

planned workout_____

_____

_____

weather_____

route_____

_____

_____

_____

dist._____time_____

zone 1_____2_____3_____4_____5_____

avg. HR_____avg. power_____

workout rating_____

notes _____

_____

_____

_____

_____

_____

_____

_____

_____

nutrition _____

_____

_____

_____

_____

TUESDAY_____/_____/_____

☐ sleep ☐ fatigue ☐ stress ☐ soreness

resting heart rate_____weight_____

planned workout_____

_____

_____

weather_____

route_____

_____

_____

_____

dist._____time_____

zone 1_____2_____3_____4_____5_____

avg. HR_____avg. power_____

workout rating_____

notes _____

_____

_____

_____

_____

_____

_____

_____

_____

nutrition _____

_____

_____

_____

_____

week goals: ▪ _____
▪ _____
▪ _____

WEDNESDAY ___/___/___   notes _____

▪ sleep ▪ fatigue ▪ stress ▪ soreness   _____

resting heart rate_____weight_____   _____

planned workout_____   _____

_____   _____

_____   _____

weather_____   _____

route_____   _____

_____   _____

_____   _____

_____   _____

dist._____time_____   ## nutrition _____

zone 1_____2_____3_____4_____5_____   _____

avg. HR_____avg. power_____   _____

workout rating_____   _____

THURSDAY ___/___/___   notes _____

▪ sleep ▪ fatigue ▪ stress ▪ soreness   _____

resting heart rate_____weight_____   _____

planned workout_____   _____

_____   _____

_____   _____

weather_____   _____

route_____   _____

_____   _____

_____   _____

_____   _____

dist._____time_____   ## nutrition _____

zone 1_____2_____3_____4_____5_____   _____

avg. HR_____avg. power_____   _____

workout rating_____   _____

FRIDAY _____/_____/_____

■ sleep ■ fatigue ■ stress ■ soreness

resting heart rate_____weight_____

planned workout_____

_____

_____

weather_____

route_____

_____

_____

_____

_____

dist._____time_____

zone 1_____2_____3_____4_____5_____

avg. HR_____avg. power_____

workout rating_____

notes _____

_____

_____

_____

_____

_____

_____

_____

_____

nutrition _____

_____

_____

_____

_____

SATURDAY _____/_____/_____

■ sleep ■ fatigue ■ stress ■ soreness

resting heart rate_____weight_____

planned workout_____

_____

weather_____

route_____

_____

_____

_____

dist._____time_____

zone 1_____2_____3_____4_____5_____

avg. HR_____avg. power_____

workout rating_____

notes _____

_____

_____

_____

_____

_____

_____

_____

nutrition _____

_____

_____

_____

_____

SUNDAY _____ / _____ / _____

■ sleep ■ fatigue ■ stress ■ soreness

resting heart rate_____weight_____

planned workout_____

_____

_____

weather_____

route_____

_____

_____

_____

dist._____time_____

zone 1_____2_____3_____4_____5_____

avg. HR_____avg. power_____

workout rating_____

notes _____

_____

_____

_____

_____

_____

_____

_____

_____

nutrition _____

_____

_____

_____

_____

RACING

race 1 _____

category_____

distance_____time _____

result _____upgrade pts. _____

notes _____

_____

_____

_____

race 2 _____

category_____

distance_____time _____

result _____upgrade pts. _____

notes _____

_____

_____

WEEKLY SUMMARY

	weekly total	YTD
bike time		
bike miles		
strength time		
total		

soreness _____

notes _____

_____

_____

_____

_____

_____

_____

_____

Period: _____   Planned Hours: _____

MONDAY _____/_____/_____

■ sleep ■ fatigue ■ stress ■ soreness

resting heart rate_____weight_____

planned workout_____

_____

_____

weather_____

route_____

_____

_____

_____

dist._____time_____

zone 1_____2_____3_____4_____5_____

avg. HR_____avg. power_____

workout rating_____

notes _____

_____

_____

_____

_____

_____

_____

_____

_____

nutrition _____

_____

_____

_____

_____

TUESDAY_____/_____/_____

■ sleep ■ fatigue ■ stress ■ soreness

resting heart rate_____weight_____

planned workout_____

_____

_____

weather_____

route_____

_____

_____

_____

dist._____time_____

zone 1_____2_____3_____4_____5_____

avg. HR_____avg. power_____

workout rating_____

notes _____

_____

_____

_____

_____

_____

_____

_____

nutrition _____

_____

_____

week goals: ■ _____
■ _____
■ _____

WEDNESDAY ____/____/____

■ sleep ■ fatigue ■ stress ■ soreness

resting heart rate_____weight_____

planned workout_____

_____

_____

weather_____

route_____

_____

_____

_____

dist._____time_____

zone 1_____2_____3_____4_____5_____

avg. HR_____avg. power_____

workout rating_____

notes _____

_____

_____

_____

_____

_____

_____

_____

_____

_____

nutrition _____

_____

_____

_____

_____

THURSDAY ____/____/____

■ sleep ■ fatigue ■ stress ■ soreness

resting heart rate_____weight_____

planned workout_____

_____

_____

weather_____

route_____

_____

_____

_____

dist._____time_____

zone 1_____2_____3_____4_____5_____

avg. HR_____avg. power_____

workout rating_____

notes _____

_____

_____

_____

_____

_____

_____

_____

_____

_____

nutrition _____

_____

_____

_____

_____

FRIDAY _____/_____/_____

■ sleep ■ fatigue ■ stress ■ soreness

resting heart rate_____weight_____

planned workout_____

_____

_____

weather_____

route_____

_____

_____

_____

dist._____time_____

zone 1_____2_____3_____4_____5_____

avg. HR_____avg. power_____

workout rating_____

_____

_____

_____

_____

_____

_____

_____

_____

nutrition _____

_____

_____

_____

_____

SATURDAY_____/_____/_____

■ sleep ■ fatigue ■ stress ■ soreness

resting heart rate_____weight_____

planned workout_____

_____

_____

weather_____

route_____

_____

_____

_____

dist._____time_____

zone 1_____2_____3_____4_____5_____

avg. HR_____avg. power_____

workout rating_____

notes _____

_____

_____

_____

_____

_____

_____

_____

nutrition _____

_____

_____

_____

_____

SUNDAY _____/_____/_____

◼ sleep ◼ fatigue ◼ stress ◼ soreness

resting heart rate_____weight_____

planned workout_____

_____

_____

weather_____

route_____

_____

_____

_____

dist._____time_____

zone 1_____2_____3_____4_____5_____

avg. HR_____avg. power_____

workout rating_____

notes _____

_____

_____

_____

_____

_____

_____

_____

nutrition _____

_____

_____

_____

_____

_____

RACING

race 1 _____

category_____

distance_____time _____

result _____upgrade pts. _____

notes _____

_____

_____

_____

race 2 _____

category_____

distance_____time _____

result _____upgrade pts. _____

notes _____

_____

_____

_____

WEEKLY SUMMARY

	weekly total	YTD
bike time		
bike miles		
strength time		
total		

soreness _____

notes _____

_____

_____

_____

_____

_____

_____

Period: _____   **Planned Hours:** _____

MONDAY _____/_____/_____

■ sleep ■ fatigue ■ stress ■ soreness

resting heart rate_____weight_____

planned workout_____

_____

_____

weather_____

route_____

_____

_____

_____

dist._____time_____

zone 1_____2_____3_____4_____5_____

avg. HR_____avg. power_____

workout rating_____

notes _____

_____

_____

_____

_____

_____

_____

_____

nutrition _____

_____

_____

_____

_____

TUESDAY_____/_____/_____

■ sleep ■ fatigue ■ stress ■ soreness

resting heart rate_____weight_____

planned workout_____

_____

_____

weather_____

route_____

_____

_____

_____

dist._____time_____

zone 1_____2_____3_____4_____5_____

avg. HR_____avg. power_____

workout rating_____

notes _____

_____

_____

_____

_____

_____

_____

_____

nutrition _____

_____

_____

_____

_____

week goals: ■ _____
■ _____
■ _____

WEDNESDAY____/____/____

■ sleep ■ fatigue ■ stress ■ soreness

resting heart rate_____weight_____

planned workout_____
_____
_____

weather_____
route_____
_____
_____
_____

dist._____time_____

zone 1_____2_____3_____4_____5_____

avg. HR_____avg. power_____

workout rating_____

notes _____
_____
_____
_____
_____
_____
_____
_____
_____
_____

nutrition _____
_____
_____
_____
_____

THURSDAY____/____/____

■ sleep ■ fatigue ■ stress ■ soreness

resting heart rate_____weight_____

planned workout_____
_____
_____

weather_____
route_____
_____
_____
_____

dist._____time_____

zone 1_____2_____3_____4_____5_____

avg. HR_____avg. power_____

workout rating_____

notes _____
_____
_____
_____
_____
_____
_____
_____
_____
_____

nutrition _____
_____
_____
_____
_____

FRIDAY _____/_____/_____

▪ sleep ▪ fatigue ▪ stress ▪ soreness

resting heart rate_____weight_____

planned workout_____

_____

_____

weather_____

route_____

_____

_____

_____

_____

dist._____time_____

zone 1_____2_____3_____4_____5_____

avg. HR_____avg. power_____

workout rating_____

notes _____

_____

_____

_____

_____

_____

_____

_____

_____

nutrition _____

_____

_____

_____

_____

_____

SATURDAY_____/_____/_____

▪ sleep ▪ fatigue ▪ stress ▪ soreness

resting heart rate_____weight_____

planned workout_____

_____

_____

weather_____

route_____

_____

_____

_____

_____

dist._____time_____

zone 1_____2_____3_____4_____5_____

avg. HR_____avg. power_____

workout rating_____

notes _____

_____

_____

_____

_____

_____

_____

_____

_____

nutrition _____

_____

_____

_____

_____

SUNDAY _____/_____/_____

■ sleep ■ fatigue ■ stress ■ soreness

resting heart rate_____weight_____

planned workout_____

_____

_____

weather_____

route_____

_____

_____

_____

_____

dist._____time_____

zone 1_____2_____3_____4_____5_____

avg. HR_____avg. power_____

workout rating_____

notes _____

_____

_____

_____

_____

_____

_____

_____

_____

nutrition _____

_____

_____

_____

_____

RACING

race 1 _____

category_____

distance_____time _____

result _____upgrade pts. _____

notes _____

_____

_____

_____

race 2 _____

category_____

distance_____time _____

result _____upgrade pts. _____

notes _____

_____

_____

WEEKLY SUMMARY

	weekly total	YTD
bike time		
bike miles		
strength time		
total		

soreness _____

notes _____

_____

_____

_____

_____

_____

_____

Period: _____

Planned Hours: _____

MONDAY _____/_____/_____

◻ sleep ◻ fatigue ◻ stress ◻ soreness

resting heart rate_____weight_____

planned workout_____

_____

_____

weather_____

route_____

_____

_____

dist._____time_____

zone 1_____2_____3_____4_____5_____

avg. HR_____avg. power_____

workout rating_____

notes _____

_____

_____

_____

_____

_____

_____

_____

_____

nutrition _____

_____

_____

_____

TUESDAY _____/_____/_____

◻ sleep ◻ fatigue ◻ stress ◻ soreness

resting heart rate_____weight_____

planned workout_____

_____

_____

weather_____

route_____

_____

_____

dist._____time_____

zone 1_____2_____3_____4_____5_____

avg. HR_____avg. power_____

workout rating_____

notes _____

_____

_____

_____

_____

_____

_____

nutrition _____

_____

_____

_____

week goals: ■ _____

■ _____

■ _____

WEDNESDAY____/____/____

■ sleep ■ fatigue ■ stress ■ soreness

resting heart rate_____weight_____

planned workout_____

_____

_____

weather_____

route_____

_____

_____

_____

dist._____time_____

zone 1_____2_____3_____4_____5_____

avg. HR_____avg. power_____

workout rating_____

notes _____

_____

_____

_____

_____

_____

_____

_____

nutrition _____

_____

_____

_____

_____

THURSDAY____/____/____

■ sleep ■ fatigue ■ stress ■ soreness

resting heart rate_____weight_____

planned workout_____

_____

_____

weather_____

route_____

_____

_____

_____

dist._____time_____

zone 1_____2_____3_____4_____5_____

avg. HR_____avg. power_____

workout rating_____

notes _____

_____

_____

_____

_____

_____

_____

_____

nutrition _____

_____

_____

_____

_____

FRIDAY_____/_____/_____

☐ sleep ☐ fatigue ☐ stress ☐ soreness

resting heart rate_____weight_____

planned workout_____

_____

_____

weather_____

route_____

_____

_____

_____

_____

dist._____time_____

zone 1_____2_____3_____4_____5_____

avg. HR_____avg. power_____

workout rating_____

notes _____

_____

_____

_____

_____

_____

_____

nutrition _____

_____

_____

_____

SATURDAY_____/_____/_____

☐ sleep ☐ fatigue ☐ stress ☐ soreness

resting heart rate_____weight_____

planned workout_____

_____

_____

weather_____

route_____

_____

_____

_____

_____

dist._____time_____

zone 1_____2_____3_____4_____5_____

avg. HR_____avg. power_____

workout rating_____

notes _____

_____

_____

_____

_____

_____

_____

nutrition _____

_____

_____

_____

SUNDAY _____/_____/_____

sleep ▪ fatigue ▪ stress ▪ soreness

resting heart rate_____weight_____

planned workout_____

_____

_____

weather_____

route_____

_____

_____

_____

dist._____time_____

zone 1_____2_____3_____4_____5_____

avg. HR_____avg. power_____

workout rating_____

notes _____

_____

_____

_____

_____

_____

_____

_____

nutrition _____

_____

_____

_____

_____

RACING

race 1 _____

category_____

distance_____time_____

result _____upgrade pts._____

notes _____

_____

_____

_____

race 2 _____

category_____

distance_____time_____

result _____upgrade pts._____

notes _____

_____

_____

WEEKLY SUMMARY

	weekly total	YTD
bike time		
bike miles		
strength time		
total		

soreness_____

notes _____

_____

_____

_____

_____

_____

Period: _____   **Planned Hours:** _____

MONDAY _____/_____/_____

☐ sleep ☐ fatigue ☐ stress ☐ soreness

resting heart rate_____weight_____

planned workout_____

_____

_____

weather_____

route_____

_____

_____

_____

dist._____time_____

zone 1_____2_____3_____4_____5_____

avg. HR_____avg. power_____

workout rating_____

notes _____

_____

_____

_____

_____

_____

_____

_____

nutrition _____

_____

_____

_____

_____

TUESDAY_____/_____/_____

☐ sleep ☐ fatigue ☐ stress ☐ soreness

resting heart rate_____weight_____

planned workout_____

_____

_____

weather_____

route_____

_____

_____

_____

dist._____time_____

zone 1_____2_____3_____4_____5_____

avg. HR_____avg. power_____

workout rating_____

notes _____

_____

_____

_____

_____

_____

_____

_____

nutrition _____

_____

_____

_____

_____

week goals: ■ _____

■ _____

■ _____

WEDNESDAY ____/____/____

■ sleep ■ fatigue ■ stress ■ soreness

resting heart rate_____weight_____

planned workout_____

_____

_____

weather_____

route_____

_____

_____

_____

dist._____time_____

zone 1_____2_____3_____4_____5_____

avg. HR_____avg. power_____

workout rating_____

notes _____

_____

_____

_____

_____

_____

_____

_____

_____

nutrition _____

_____

_____

_____

_____

THURSDAY ____/____/____

■ sleep ■ fatigue ■ stress ■ soreness

resting heart rate_____weight_____

planned workout_____

_____

_____

weather_____

route_____

_____

_____

_____

dist._____time_____

zone 1_____2_____3_____4_____5_____

avg. HR_____avg. power_____

workout rating_____

notes _____

_____

_____

_____

_____

_____

_____

_____

_____

nutrition _____

_____

_____

_____

FRIDAY _____/_____/_____

■ sleep ■ fatigue ■ stress ■ soreness

resting heart rate_____weight_____

planned workout_____

_____

_____

weather_____

route_____

_____

_____

_____

_____

dist._____time_____

zone 1_____2_____3_____4_____5_____

avg. HR_____avg. power_____

workout rating_____

notes _____

_____

_____

_____

_____

_____

_____

_____

nutrition _____

_____

_____

_____

_____

SATURDAY_____/_____/_____

■ sleep ■ fatigue ■ stress ■ soreness

resting heart rate_____weight_____

planned workout_____

_____

_____

weather_____

route_____

_____

_____

_____

_____

dist._____time_____

zone 1_____2_____3_____4_____5_____

avg. HR_____avg. power_____

workout rating_____

notes _____

_____

_____

_____

_____

_____

_____

nutrition _____

_____

_____

_____

SUNDAY _____/_____/_____

sleep   fatigue   stress   soreness

resting heart rate_____weight_____

planned workout_____

_____

_____

weather_____

route_____

_____

_____

_____

_____

dist._____time_____

zone 1_____2_____3_____4_____5_____

avg. HR_____avg. power_____

workout rating_____

notes _____

_____

_____

_____

_____

_____

_____

_____

_____

nutrition _____

_____

_____

_____

RACING

race 1 _____

category_____

distance_____time _____

result _____upgrade pts. _____

notes _____

_____

_____

_____

race 2 _____

category_____

distance_____time _____

result _____upgrade pts. _____

notes _____

_____

_____

_____

WEEKLY SUMMARY

	weekly total	YTD
bike time		
bike miles		
strength time		
total		

soreness _____

notes _____

_____

_____

_____

_____

_____

_____

_____

Period: _____   **Planned Hours:** _____

MONDAY _____/_____/_____

☐ sleep   ☐ fatigue   ☐ stress   ☐ soreness

resting heart rate_____weight_____

planned workout_____

_____

_____

weather_____

route_____

_____

_____

_____

dist._____time_____

zone 1_____2_____3_____4_____5_____

avg. HR_____avg. power_____

workout rating_____

notes _____

_____

_____

_____

_____

_____

_____

_____

_____

nutrition _____

_____

_____

_____

_____

TUESDAY_____/_____/_____

☐ sleep   ☐ fatigue   ☐ stress   ☐ soreness

resting heart rate_____weight_____

planned workout_____

_____

_____

weather_____

route_____

_____

_____

dist._____time_____

zone 1_____2_____3_____4_____5_____

avg. HR_____avg. power_____

workout rating_____

notes _____

_____

_____

_____

_____

_____

_____

_____

nutrition _____

_____

_____

_____

week goals: ▪ _____
▪ _____
▪ _____

WEDNESDAY___/___/___   **notes** _____

▪ sleep ▪ fatigue ▪ stress ▪ soreness   _____

resting heart rate_____weight_____   _____

planned workout_____   _____

_____   _____

_____   _____

weather_____   _____

route_____   _____

_____   _____

_____   _____

_____   _____

dist._____time_____   **nutrition** _____

zone 1_____2_____3_____4_____5_____   _____

avg. HR_____avg. power_____   _____

workout rating_____   _____

_____   _____

THURSDAY___/___/___   **notes** _____

▪ sleep ▪ fatigue ▪ stress ▪ soreness   _____

resting heart rate_____weight_____   _____

planned workout_____   _____

_____   _____

_____   _____

weather_____   _____

route_____   _____

_____   _____

_____   _____

_____   _____

dist._____time_____   **nutrition** _____

zone 1_____2_____3_____4_____5_____   _____

avg. HR_____avg. power_____   _____

workout rating_____   _____

_____   _____

FRIDAY _____/_____/_____

■ sleep ■ fatigue ■ stress ■ soreness

resting heart rate_____weight_____

planned workout_____

_____

_____

weather_____

route_____

_____

_____

_____

_____

dist._____time_____

zone 1_____2_____3_____4_____5_____

avg. HR_____avg. power_____

workout rating_____

notes _____

_____

_____

_____

_____

_____

_____

_____

_____

nutrition _____

_____

_____

_____

_____

SATURDAY_____/_____/_____

■ sleep ■ fatigue ■ stress ■ soreness

resting heart rate_____weight_____

planned workout_____

_____

_____

weather_____

route_____

_____

_____

_____

_____

dist._____time_____

zone 1_____2_____3_____4_____5_____

avg. HR_____avg. power_____

workout rating_____

notes _____

_____

_____

_____

_____

_____

_____

_____

_____

nutrition _____

_____

_____

_____

_____

SUNDAY _____/_____/_____

☐ sleep ☐ fatigue ☐ stress ☐ soreness

resting heart rate_____weight_____

planned workout_____

_____

_____

weather_____

route_____

_____

_____

_____

dist._____time_____

zone 1_____2_____3_____4_____5_____

avg. HR_____avg. power_____

workout rating_____

RACING

race 1 _____

category_____

distance_____time_____

result _____upgrade pts. _____

notes _____

_____

_____

race 2 _____

category_____

distance_____time_____

result _____upgrade pts. _____

notes _____

_____

_____

notes _____

_____

_____

_____

_____

_____

_____

_____

nutrition _____

_____

_____

_____

WEEKLY SUMMARY

	weekly total	YTD
bike time		
bike miles		
strength time		
total		

soreness _____

notes _____

_____

_____

_____

_____

_____

_____

Period: _____ **Planned Hours:** _____

MONDAY _____/_____/_____

☐ sleep ☐ fatigue ☐ stress ☐ soreness

resting heart rate_____weight_____

planned workout_____

_____

_____

weather_____

route_____

_____

_____

dist._____time_____

zone 1_____2_____3_____4_____5_____

avg. HR_____avg. power_____

workout rating_____

notes _____

_____

_____

_____

_____

_____

_____

_____

_____

nutrition _____

_____

_____

_____

_____

TUESDAY_____/_____/_____

☐ sleep ☐ fatigue ☐ stress ☐ soreness

resting heart rate_____weight_____

planned workout_____

_____

_____

weather_____

route_____

_____

_____

dist._____time_____

zone 1_____2_____3_____4_____5_____

avg. HR_____avg. power_____

workout rating_____

notes _____

_____

_____

_____

_____

_____

_____

_____

_____

nutrition _____

_____

_____

_____

_____

week goals: ■ _____
■ _____
■ _____

WEDNESDAY____/____/____

■ sleep ■ fatigue ■ stress ■ soreness

resting heart rate_____weight_____

planned workout_____

_____

_____

weather_____

route_____

_____

_____

_____

dist._____time_____

zone 1_____2_____3_____4_____5_____

avg. HR_____avg. power_____

workout rating_____

notes _____
_____
_____
_____
_____
_____
_____
_____
_____
_____

nutrition _____
_____
_____
_____
_____

THURSDAY____/____/____

■ sleep ■ fatigue ■ stress ■ soreness

resting heart rate_____weight_____

planned workout_____

_____

_____

weather_____

route_____

_____

_____

_____

dist._____time_____

zone 1_____2_____3_____4_____5_____

avg. HR_____avg. power_____

workout rating_____

notes _____
_____
_____
_____
_____
_____
_____
_____
_____
_____

nutrition _____
_____
_____
_____
_____

FRIDAY_____/_____/_____

☐ sleep ☐ fatigue ☐ stress ☐ soreness

resting heart rate_____weight_____

planned workout_____

_____

_____

weather_____

route_____

_____

_____

_____

_____

dist._____time_____

zone 1_____2_____3_____4_____5_____

avg. HR_____avg. power_____

workout rating_____

notes _____

_____

_____

_____

_____

_____

_____

_____

_____

_____

nutrition _____

_____

_____

_____

SATURDAY_____/_____/_____

☐ sleep ☐ fatigue ☐ stress ☐ soreness

resting heart rate_____weight_____

planned workout_____

_____

_____

weather_____

route_____

_____

_____

_____

_____

dist._____time_____

zone 1_____2_____3_____4_____5_____

avg. HR_____avg. power_____

workout rating_____

notes _____

_____

_____

_____

_____

_____

_____

_____

_____

_____

nutrition _____

_____

_____

_____

SUNDAY _____/_____/_____

■ sleep ■ fatigue ■ stress ■ soreness

resting heart rate_____weight_____

planned workout_____

_____

_____

weather_____

route_____

_____

_____

_____

_____

dist._____time_____

zone 1_____2_____3_____4_____5_____

avg. HR_____avg. power_____

workout rating_____

notes _____

_____

_____

_____

_____

_____

_____

_____

_____

nutrition _____

_____

_____

_____

RACING

race 1 _____

category_____

distance_____time _____

result _____upgrade pts. _____

notes _____

_____

_____

_____

race 2 _____

category_____

distance_____time _____

result _____upgrade pts. _____

notes _____

_____

_____

WEEKLY SUMMARY

	weekly total	YTD
bike time		
bike miles		
strength time		
total		
soreness		

notes _____

_____

_____

_____

_____

_____

week beginning:

Period: _____   **Planned Hours:** _____

MONDAY _____/_____/_____

☐ sleep ☐ fatigue ☐ stress ☐ soreness

resting heart rate_____weight_____

planned workout_____

_____

_____

weather_____

route_____

_____

_____

_____

dist._____time_____

zone 1_____2_____3_____4_____5_____

avg. HR_____avg. power_____

workout rating_____

notes _____

_____

_____

_____

_____

_____

_____

_____

_____

nutrition _____

_____

_____

_____

_____

TUESDAY_____/_____/_____

☐ sleep ☐ fatigue ☐ stress ☐ soreness

resting heart rate_____weight_____

planned workout_____

_____

_____

weather_____

route_____

_____

_____

_____

dist._____time_____

zone 1_____2_____3_____4_____5_____

avg. HR_____avg. power_____

workout rating_____

notes _____

_____

_____

_____

_____

_____

_____

_____

_____

nutrition _____

_____

_____

_____

_____

week goals: ▪ _____
▪ _____
▪ _____

WEDNESDAY ____/____/____

▪ sleep ▪ fatigue ▪ stress ▪ soreness

resting heart rate_____weight_____

planned workout_____

_____

_____

weather_____

route_____

_____

_____

_____

dist._____time_____

zone 1_____2_____3_____4_____5_____

avg. HR_____avg. power_____

workout rating_____

notes _____

_____

_____

_____

_____

_____

_____

_____

_____

_____

_____

nutrition _____

_____

_____

_____

_____

THURSDAY ____/____/____

▪ sleep ▪ fatigue ▪ stress ▪ soreness

resting heart rate_____weight_____

planned workout_____

_____

weather_____

route_____

_____

_____

_____

dist._____time_____

zone 1_____2_____3_____4_____5_____

avg. HR_____avg. power_____

workout rating_____

notes _____

_____

_____

_____

_____

_____

_____

_____

_____

_____

nutrition _____

_____

_____

_____

_____

FRIDAY _____ / _____ / _____

☐ sleep ☐ fatigue ☐ stress ☐ soreness

resting heart rate_____weight_____

planned workout_____

_____

_____

weather_____

route_____

_____

_____

_____

_____

dist._____time_____

zone 1_____2_____3_____4_____5_____

avg. HR_____avg. power_____

workout rating_____

notes _____

_____

_____

_____

_____

_____

_____

_____

_____

nutrition _____

_____

_____

_____

SATURDAY _____ / _____ / _____

☐ sleep ☐ fatigue ☐ stress ☐ soreness

resting heart rate_____weight_____

planned workout_____

_____

_____

weather_____

route_____

_____

_____

_____

_____

dist._____time_____

zone 1_____2_____3_____4_____5_____

avg. HR_____avg. power_____

workout rating_____

notes _____

_____

_____

_____

_____

_____

_____

_____

_____

nutrition _____

_____

_____

_____

SUNDAY _____/_____/_____

☐ sleep ☐ fatigue ☐ stress ☐ soreness

resting heart rate_____weight_____

planned workout_____

_____

_____

weather_____

route_____

_____

_____

_____

_____

dist._____time_____

zone 1_____2_____3_____4_____5_____

avg. HR_____avg. power_____

workout rating_____

notes _____

_____

_____

_____

_____

_____

_____

_____

_____

_____

_____

nutrition _____

_____

_____

_____

RACING

race 1 _____

category_____

distance_____time _____

result _____upgrade pts. _____

notes _____

_____

_____

_____

race 2 _____

category_____

distance_____time _____

result _____upgrade pts. _____

notes _____

_____

_____

_____

WEEKLY SUMMARY

	weekly total	YTD
bike time		
bike miles		
strength time		
total		

soreness_____

notes _____

_____

_____

_____

_____

_____

_____

Period: _____

Planned Hours: _____

MONDAY _____/_____/_____

◼ sleep ◼ fatigue ◼ stress ◼ soreness

resting heart rate_____weight_____

planned workout_____

_____

_____

weather_____

route_____

_____

_____

_____

dist._____time_____

zone 1_____2_____3_____4_____5_____

avg. HR_____avg. power_____

workout rating_____

notes _____

_____

_____

_____

_____

_____

_____

_____

_____

nutrition _____

_____

_____

_____

_____

TUESDAY_____/_____/_____

◼ sleep ◼ fatigue ◼ stress ◼ soreness

resting heart rate_____weight_____

planned workout_____

_____

_____

weather_____

route_____

_____

_____

_____

dist._____time_____

zone 1_____2_____3_____4_____5_____

avg. HR_____avg. power_____

workout rating_____

notes _____

_____

_____

_____

_____

_____

_____

_____

_____

nutrition _____

_____

_____

_____

_____

week goals: ■ _____
■ _____
■ _____

WEDNESDAY___/___/___   **notes** _____
■ sleep ■ fatigue ■ stress ■ soreness   _____
resting heart rate_____weight_____   _____
planned workout_____   _____
_____   _____
_____   _____
weather_____   _____
route_____   _____
_____   _____
_____   _____
_____   _____
dist._____time_____   **nutrition** _____
zone 1____2____3____4____5____   _____
avg. HR_____avg. power_____   _____
workout rating_____   _____

THURSDAY___/___/___   **notes** _____
■ sleep ■ fatigue ■ stress ■ soreness   _____
resting heart rate_____weight_____   _____
planned workout_____   _____
_____   _____
_____   _____
weather_____   _____
route_____   _____
_____   _____
_____   _____
_____   _____
dist._____time_____   **nutrition** _____
zone 1____2____3____4____5____   _____
avg. HR_____avg. power_____   _____
workout rating_____   _____

FRIDAY_____/_____/_____

▪ sleep ▪ fatigue ▪ stress ▪ soreness

resting heart rate_____weight_____

planned workout_____

_____

_____

weather_____

route_____

_____

_____

_____

_____

dist._____time_____

zone 1_____2_____3_____4_____5_____

avg. HR_____avg. power_____

workout rating_____

notes _____

_____

_____

_____

_____

_____

_____

_____

_____

nutrition _____

_____

_____

_____

_____

_____

SATURDAY_____/_____/_____

▪ sleep ▪ fatigue ▪ stress ▪ soreness

resting heart rate_____weight_____

planned workout_____

_____

_____

weather_____

route_____

_____

_____

_____

_____

dist._____time_____

zone 1_____2_____3_____4_____5_____

avg. HR_____avg. power_____

workout rating_____

notes _____

_____

_____

_____

_____

_____

_____

_____

_____

nutrition _____

_____

_____

_____

_____

SUNDAY _____ / _____ / _____

■ sleep ■ fatigue ■ stress ■ soreness

resting heart rate _____ weight _____

planned workout _____

_____

_____

weather _____

route _____

_____

_____

_____

_____

dist. _____ time _____

zone 1 _____ 2 _____ 3 _____ 4 _____ 5 _____

avg. HR _____ avg. power _____

workout rating _____

notes _____

_____

_____

_____

_____

_____

_____

_____

_____

_____

nutrition _____

_____

_____

_____

_____

RACING

race 1 _____

category _____

distance _____ time _____

result _____ upgrade pts. _____

notes _____

_____

_____

_____

race 2 _____

category _____

distance _____ time _____

result _____ upgrade pts. _____

notes _____

_____

_____

_____

WEEKLY SUMMARY

	weekly total	YTD
bike time		
bike miles		
strength time		
total		

soreness _____

notes _____

_____

_____

_____

_____

_____

_____

_____

Period: _____   **Planned Hours:** _____

MONDAY _____/_____/_____

▪ sleep ▪ fatigue ▪ stress ▪ soreness

resting heart rate_____weight_____

planned workout_____

_____

_____

weather_____

route_____

_____

_____

_____

dist._____time_____

zone 1_____2_____3_____4_____5_____

avg. HR_____avg. power_____

workout rating_____

notes _____

_____

_____

_____

_____

_____

_____

_____

_____

nutrition _____

_____

_____

_____

_____

TUESDAY_____/_____/_____

▪ sleep ▪ fatigue ▪ stress ▪ soreness

resting heart rate_____weight_____

planned workout_____

_____

_____

weather_____

route_____

_____

_____

_____

dist._____time_____

zone 1_____2_____3_____4_____5_____

avg. HR_____avg. power_____

workout rating_____

notes _____

_____

_____

_____

_____

_____

_____

_____

_____

nutrition _____

_____

_____

_____

_____

week goals: ▪ _____

▪ _____

▪ _____

WEDNESDAY____/____/____   notes _____

▪ sleep ▪ fatigue ▪ stress ▪ soreness

resting heart rate_____weight_____

planned workout_____

_____

_____

weather_____

route_____

_____

_____

_____

dist._____time_____   **nutrition** _____

zone 1_____2_____3_____4_____5_____

avg. HR_____avg. power_____

workout rating_____

THURSDAY____/____/____   notes _____

▪ sleep ▪ fatigue ▪ stress ▪ soreness

resting heart rate_____weight_____

planned workout_____

_____

_____

weather_____

route_____

_____

_____

_____

dist._____time_____   **nutrition** _____

zone 1_____2_____3_____4_____5_____

avg. HR_____avg. power_____

workout rating_____

FRIDAY _____ / _____ / _____

▨ sleep ▨ fatigue ▨ stress ▨ soreness

resting heart rate_____weight_____

planned workout_____

_____

weather_____

route_____

_____

_____

_____

_____

dist._____time_____

zone 1_____2_____3_____4_____5_____

avg. HR_____avg. power_____

workout rating_____

notes _____

_____

_____

_____

_____

_____

_____

_____

nutrition _____

_____

_____

_____

_____

SATURDAY _____ / _____ / _____

▨ sleep ▨ fatigue ▨ stress ▨ soreness

resting heart rate_____weight_____

planned workout_____

_____

weather_____

route_____

_____

_____

_____

_____

dist._____time_____

zone 1_____2_____3_____4_____5_____

avg. HR_____avg. power_____

workout rating_____

notes _____

_____

_____

_____

_____

_____

_____

_____

nutrition _____

_____

_____

_____

_____

SUNDAY_____/_____/_____

■ sleep ■ fatigue ■ stress ■ soreness

resting heart rate_____weight_____

planned workout_____

_____

_____

weather_____

route_____

_____

_____

_____

_____

dist._____time_____

zone 1_____2_____3_____4_____5_____

avg. HR_____avg. power_____

workout rating_____

notes _____

_____

_____

_____

_____

_____

_____

_____

_____

_____

nutrition _____

_____

_____

_____

RACING

race 1 _____

category_____

distance_____time _____

result _____upgrade pts. _____

notes _____

_____

_____

_____

race 2 _____

category_____

distance_____time _____

result _____upgrade pts. _____

notes _____

_____

_____

_____

WEEKLY SUMMARY

	weekly total	YTD
bike time		
bike miles		
strength time		
total		

soreness _____

notes _____

_____

_____

_____

_____

_____

_____

Period: _____   **Planned Hours:** _____

MONDAY _____/_____/_____

■ sleep   ■ fatigue   ■ stress   ■ soreness

resting heart rate_____weight_____

planned workout_____

_____

_____

weather_____

route_____

_____

_____

_____

dist._____time_____

zone 1_____2_____3_____4_____5_____

avg. HR_____avg. power_____

workout rating_____

notes _____

_____

_____

_____

_____

_____

_____

_____

nutrition _____

_____

_____

_____

TUESDAY_____/_____/_____

■ sleep   ■ fatigue   ■ stress   ■ soreness

resting heart rate_____weight_____

planned workout_____

_____

_____

weather_____

route_____

_____

_____

_____

dist._____time_____

zone 1_____2_____3_____4_____5_____

avg. HR_____avg. power_____

workout rating_____

notes _____

_____

_____

_____

_____

_____

_____

_____

nutrition _____

_____

_____

_____

week goals: ■ _____

■ _____

■ _____

WEDNESDAY___/___/___

■ sleep   ■ fatigue   ■ stress   ■ soreness

resting heart rate_____weight_____

planned workout_____

_____

_____

weather_____

route_____

_____

_____

_____

dist._____time_____

zone 1_____2_____3_____4_____5_____

avg. HR_____avg. power_____

workout rating_____

notes _____

_____

_____

_____

_____

_____

_____

_____

_____

_____

_____

_____

nutrition _____

_____

_____

_____

_____

THURSDAY___/___/___

■ sleep   ■ fatigue   ■ stress   ■ soreness

resting heart rate_____weight_____

planned workout_____

_____

_____

weather_____

route_____

_____

_____

_____

dist._____time_____

zone 1_____2_____3_____4_____5_____

avg. HR_____avg. power_____

workout rating_____

notes _____

_____

_____

_____

_____

_____

_____

_____

_____

_____

_____

_____

nutrition _____

_____

_____

_____

_____

FRIDAY _____/_____/_____

☐ sleep ☐ fatigue ☐ stress ☐ soreness

resting heart rate_____weight_____

planned workout_____

_____

_____

weather_____

route_____

_____

_____

_____

dist._____time_____

zone 1_____2_____3_____4_____5_____

avg. HR_____avg. power_____

workout rating_____

notes _____

_____

_____

_____

_____

_____

_____

_____

_____

nutrition _____

_____

_____

_____

_____

SATURDAY _____/_____/_____

☐ sleep ☐ fatigue ☐ stress ☐ soreness

resting heart rate_____weight_____

planned workout_____

_____

_____

weather_____

route_____

_____

_____

_____

dist._____time_____

zone 1_____2_____3_____4_____5_____

avg. HR_____avg. power_____

workout rating_____

notes _____

_____

_____

_____

_____

_____

_____

_____

_____

nutrition _____

_____

_____

_____

_____

SUNDAY _____/_____/_____

■ sleep ■ fatigue ■ stress ■ soreness

resting heart rate_____weight_____

planned workout_____

_____

_____

weather_____

route_____

_____

_____

_____

dist._____time_____

zone 1_____2_____3_____4_____5_____

avg. HR_____avg. power_____

workout rating_____

notes _____

_____

_____

_____

_____

_____

_____

_____

_____

nutrition _____

_____

_____

_____

RACING

race 1 _____

category_____

distance_____time _____

result _____upgrade pts. _____

notes _____

_____

_____

_____

race 2 _____

category_____

distance_____time _____

result _____upgrade pts. _____

notes _____

_____

_____

WEEKLY SUMMARY

	weekly total	YTD
bike time		
bike miles		
strength time		
total		

soreness _____

notes _____

_____

_____

_____

_____

_____

_____

Period: _____   **Planned Hours:** _____

MONDAY _____/_____/_____

☐ sleep ☐ fatigue ☐ stress ☐ soreness

resting heart rate_____weight_____

planned workout_____

_____

_____

weather_____

route_____

_____

_____

_____

dist._____time_____

zone 1_____2_____3_____4_____5_____

avg. HR_____avg. power_____

workout rating_____

notes _____

_____

_____

_____

_____

_____

_____

_____

_____

nutrition _____

_____

_____

_____

_____

TUESDAY_____/_____/_____

☐ sleep ☐ fatigue ☐ stress ☐ soreness

resting heart rate_____weight_____

planned workout_____

_____

_____

weather_____

route_____

_____

_____

_____

dist._____time_____

zone 1_____2_____3_____4_____5_____

avg. HR_____avg. power_____

workout rating_____

notes _____

_____

_____

_____

_____

_____

_____

_____

_____

nutrition _____

_____

_____

_____

_____

week goals: ▪ _____
▪ _____
▪ _____

WEDNESDAY___/___/___

▪ sleep ▪ fatigue ▪ stress ▪ soreness

resting heart rate_____weight_____

planned workout_____

_____

_____

weather_____

route_____

_____

_____

dist._____time_____

zone 1_____2_____3_____4_____5_____

avg. HR_____avg. power_____

workout rating_____

notes _____
_____
_____
_____
_____
_____
_____
_____
_____
_____

nutrition _____
_____
_____
_____
_____

THURSDAY___/___/___

▪ sleep ▪ fatigue ▪ stress ▪ soreness

resting heart rate_____weight_____

planned workout_____

_____

_____

weather_____

route_____

_____

_____

dist._____time_____

zone 1_____2_____3_____4_____5_____

avg. HR_____avg. power_____

workout rating_____

notes _____
_____
_____
_____
_____
_____
_____
_____
_____

nutrition _____
_____
_____
_____

FRIDAY _____/_____/_____

■ sleep ■ fatigue ■ stress ■ soreness

resting heart rate_____weight_____

planned workout_____

_____

_____

weather_____

route_____

_____

_____

_____

dist._____time_____

zone 1_____2_____3_____4_____5_____

avg. HR_____avg. power_____

workout rating_____

notes _____

_____

_____

_____

_____

_____

_____

_____

nutrition _____

_____

_____

_____

_____

SATURDAY_____/_____/_____

■ sleep ■ fatigue ■ stress ■ soreness

resting heart rate_____weight_____

planned workout_____

_____

_____

weather_____

route_____

_____

_____

_____

dist._____time_____

zone 1_____2_____3_____4_____5_____

avg. HR_____avg. power_____

workout rating_____

notes _____

_____

_____

_____

_____

_____

_____

_____

nutrition _____

_____

_____

_____

_____

SUNDAY _____/_____/_____

■ sleep ■ fatigue ■ stress ■ soreness

resting heart rate_____weight_____

planned workout_____

_____

_____

weather_____

route_____

_____

_____

_____

_____

dist._____time_____

zone 1_____2_____3_____4_____5_____

avg. HR_____avg. power_____

workout rating_____

notes _____

_____

_____

_____

_____

_____

_____

_____

_____

_____

nutrition _____

_____

_____

_____

RACING

race 1 _____

category_____

distance_____time _____

result _____upgrade pts._____

notes _____

_____

_____

_____

race 2 _____

category_____

distance_____time _____

result _____upgrade pts._____

notes _____

_____

_____

_____

WEEKLY SUMMARY

	weekly total	YTD
bike time		
bike miles		
strength time		
total		

soreness_____

notes _____

_____

_____

_____

_____

_____

_____

Period: _____   **Planned Hours:** _____

MONDAY _____/_____/_____

☐ sleep ☐ fatigue ☐ stress ☐ soreness

resting heart rate_____weight_____

planned workout_____

_____

_____

weather_____

route_____

_____

_____

_____

dist._____time_____

zone 1_____2_____3_____4_____5_____

avg. HR_____avg. power_____

workout rating_____

notes _____

_____

_____

_____

_____

_____

_____

_____

_____

_____

_____

nutrition _____

_____

_____

_____

_____

TUESDAY_____/_____/_____

☐ sleep ☐ fatigue ☐ stress ☐ soreness

resting heart rate_____weight_____

planned workout_____

_____

_____

weather_____

route_____

_____

_____

_____

dist._____time_____

zone 1_____2_____3_____4_____5_____

avg. HR_____avg. power_____

workout rating_____

notes _____

_____

_____

_____

_____

_____

_____

_____

_____

_____

_____

nutrition _____

_____

_____

_____

_____

week goals: ◾ _____

◾ _____

◾ _____

WEDNESDAY___/___/___

◾ sleep ◾ fatigue ◾ stress ◾ soreness

resting heart rate_____weight_____

planned workout_____

_____

_____

weather_____

route_____

_____

_____

_____

dist._____time_____

zone 1_____2_____3_____4_____5_____

avg. HR_____avg. power_____

workout rating_____

notes _____

_____

_____

_____

_____

_____

_____

_____

_____

nutrition _____

_____

_____

_____

_____

THURSDAY___/___/___

◾ sleep ◾ fatigue ◾ stress ◾ soreness

resting heart rate_____weight_____

planned workout_____

_____

_____

weather_____

route_____

_____

_____

_____

dist._____time_____

zone 1_____2_____3_____4_____5_____

avg. HR_____avg. power_____

workout rating_____

notes _____

_____

_____

_____

_____

_____

_____

_____

nutrition _____

_____

_____

_____

FRIDAY_____/_____/_____

⬜ sleep ⬜ fatigue ⬜ stress ⬜ soreness

resting heart rate_____weight_____

planned workout_____

_____

_____

weather_____

route_____

_____

_____

_____

_____

dist._____time_____

zone 1_____2_____3_____4_____5_____

avg. HR_____avg. power_____

workout rating_____

notes _____

_____

_____

_____

_____

_____

_____

_____

_____

_____

nutrition _____

_____

_____

_____

_____

SATURDAY_____/_____/_____

⬜ sleep ⬜ fatigue ⬜ stress ⬜ soreness

resting heart rate_____weight_____

planned workout_____

_____

_____

weather_____

route_____

_____

_____

_____

_____

dist._____time_____

zone 1_____2_____3_____4_____5_____

avg. HR_____avg. power_____

workout rating_____

notes _____

_____

_____

_____

_____

_____

_____

_____

_____

_____

nutrition _____

_____

_____

_____

_____

SUNDAY_____/_____/_____

⬜ sleep ⬜ fatigue ⬜ stress ⬜ soreness

resting heart rate_____weight_____

planned workout_____

_____

_____

weather_____

route_____

_____

_____

_____

dist._____time_____

zone 1_____2_____3_____4_____5_____

avg. HR_____avg. power_____

workout rating_____

notes _____

_____

_____

_____

_____

_____

_____

_____

_____

_____

nutrition _____

_____

_____

_____

_____

RACING

race 1 _____

category_____

distance_____time _____

result _____upgrade pts. _____

notes _____

_____

_____

_____

race 2 _____

category_____

distance_____time _____

result _____upgrade pts. _____

notes _____

_____

_____

WEEKLY SUMMARY

	weekly total	YTD
bike time		
bike miles		
strength time		
total		

soreness _____

notes _____

_____

_____

_____

_____

_____

Period: _____   **Planned Hours:** _____

MONDAY _____ / _____ / _____

■ sleep ■ fatigue ■ stress ■ soreness

resting heart rate_____weight_____

planned workout_____

_____

_____

weather_____

route_____

_____

_____

_____

dist._____time_____

zone 1_____2_____3_____4_____5_____

avg. HR_____avg. power_____

workout rating_____

notes _____

_____

_____

_____

_____

_____

_____

_____

_____

_____

nutrition _____

_____

_____

_____

_____

TUESDAY _____ / _____ / _____

■ sleep ■ fatigue ■ stress ■ soreness

resting heart rate_____weight_____

planned workout_____

_____

_____

weather_____

route_____

_____

_____

_____

dist._____time_____

zone 1_____2_____3_____4_____5_____

avg. HR_____avg. power_____

workout rating_____

notes _____

_____

_____

_____

_____

_____

_____

_____

_____

_____

nutrition _____

_____

_____

_____

_____

week goals: ▪ _____
▪ _____
▪ _____

WEDNESDAY___/___/___

▪ sleep ▪ fatigue ▪ stress ▪ soreness

resting heart rate_____weight_____

planned workout_____

_____

_____

weather_____

route_____

_____

_____

_____

dist._____time_____

zone 1_____2_____3_____4_____5_____

avg. HR_____avg. power_____

workout rating_____

notes _____

_____

_____

_____

_____

_____

_____

_____

_____

_____

nutrition _____

_____

_____

_____

_____

THURSDAY____/____/____

▪ sleep ▪ fatigue ▪ stress ▪ soreness

resting heart rate_____weight_____

planned workout_____

_____

_____

weather_____

route_____

_____

_____

_____

dist._____time_____

zone 1_____2_____3_____4_____5_____

avg. HR_____avg. power_____

workout rating_____

notes _____

_____

_____

_____

_____

_____

_____

_____

_____

nutrition _____

_____

_____

_____

_____

FRIDAY_____/_____/_____

 sleep fatigue stress soreness

resting heart rate_____weight_____

planned workout_____

_____

_____

weather_____

route_____

_____

_____

_____

_____

dist._____time_____

zone 1_____2_____3_____4_____5_____

avg. HR_____avg. power_____

workout rating_____

notes _____

_____

_____

_____

_____

_____

_____

_____

_____

_____

_____

nutrition _____

_____

_____

_____

SATURDAY_____/_____/_____

 sleep fatigue stress soreness

resting heart rate_____weight_____

planned workout_____

_____

_____

weather_____

route_____

_____

_____

_____

_____

dist._____time_____

zone 1_____2_____3_____4_____5_____

avg. HR_____avg. power_____

workout rating_____

notes _____

_____

_____

_____

_____

_____

_____

_____

_____

nutrition _____

_____

_____

_____

SUNDAY _____/_____/_____

☐ sleep ☐ fatigue ☐ stress ☐ soreness

resting heart rate_____weight_____

planned workout_____

_____

_____

weather_____

route_____

_____

_____

_____

_____

dist._____time_____

zone 1_____2_____3_____4_____5_____

avg. HR_____avg. power_____

workout rating_____

notes _____

_____

_____

_____

_____

_____

_____

_____

_____

_____

nutrition _____

_____

_____

_____

RACING

race 1 _____

category_____

distance_____time _____

result _____upgrade pts. _____

notes _____

_____

_____

_____

race 2 _____

category_____

distance_____time _____

result _____upgrade pts. _____

notes _____

_____

_____

WEEKLY SUMMARY

	weekly total	YTD
bike time		
bike miles		
strength time		
total		

soreness_____

notes _____

_____

_____

_____

_____

_____

Period: _____   **Planned Hours:** _____

MONDAY _____/_____/_____

▮ sleep   ▮ fatigue   ▮ stress   ▮ soreness

resting heart rate_____weight_____

planned workout_____

_____

_____

weather_____

route_____

_____

_____

_____

dist._____time_____

zone 1_____2_____3_____4_____5_____

avg. HR_____avg. power_____

workout rating_____

notes _____

_____

_____

_____

_____

_____

_____

_____

nutrition _____

_____

_____

_____

_____

TUESDAY _____/_____/_____

▮ sleep   ▮ fatigue   ▮ stress   ▮ soreness

resting heart rate_____weight_____

planned workout_____

_____

_____

weather_____

route_____

_____

_____

_____

dist._____time_____

zone 1_____2_____3_____4_____5_____

avg. HR_____avg. power_____

workout rating_____

notes _____

_____

_____

_____

_____

_____

_____

_____

nutrition _____

_____

_____

_____

_____

week goals:

■ _____

■ _____

■ _____

WEDNESDAY____/____/____

■ sleep ■ fatigue ■ stress ■ soreness

resting heart rate_____weight_____

planned workout_____

_____

_____

weather_____

route_____

_____

_____

_____

dist._____time_____

zone 1_____2_____3_____4_____5_____

avg. HR_____avg. power_____

workout rating_____

notes _____

_____

_____

_____

_____

_____

_____

_____

_____

_____

_____

nutrition _____

_____

_____

_____

THURSDAY____/____/____

■ sleep ■ fatigue ■ stress ■ soreness

resting heart rate_____weight_____

planned workout_____

_____

_____

weather_____

route_____

_____

_____

_____

dist._____time_____

zone 1_____2_____3_____4_____5_____

avg. HR_____avg. power_____

workout rating_____

notes _____

_____

_____

_____

_____

_____

_____

_____

_____

_____

_____

nutrition _____

_____

_____

_____

FRIDAY _____/_____/_____

■ sleep ■ fatigue ■ stress ■ soreness

resting heart rate_____weight_____

planned workout_____

_____

_____

weather_____

route_____

_____

_____

_____

dist._____time_____

zone 1_____2_____3_____4_____5_____

avg. HR_____avg. power_____

workout rating_____

notes _____

_____

_____

_____

_____

_____

_____

_____

_____

_____

nutrition _____

_____

_____

_____

_____

SATURDAY_____/_____/_____

■ sleep ■ fatigue ■ stress ■ soreness

resting heart rate_____weight_____

planned workout_____

_____

_____

weather_____

route_____

_____

_____

_____

dist._____time_____

zone 1_____2_____3_____4_____5_____

avg. HR_____avg. power_____

workout rating_____

notes _____

_____

_____

_____

_____

_____

_____

_____

_____

_____

nutrition _____

_____

_____

_____

_____

SUNDAY _____/_____/_____

- sleep - fatigue - stress - soreness

resting heart rate_____weight_____

planned workout_____

_____

_____

weather_____

route_____

_____

_____

_____

dist._____time_____

zone 1_____2_____3_____4_____5_____

avg. HR_____avg. power_____

workout rating_____

notes _____

_____

_____

_____

_____

_____

_____

_____

nutrition _____

_____

_____

_____

RACING

race 1 _____

category_____

distance_____time _____

result _____upgrade pts. _____

notes _____

_____

_____

_____

race 2 _____

category_____

distance_____time _____

result _____upgrade pts. _____

notes _____

_____

_____

WEEKLY SUMMARY

	weekly total	YTD
bike time		
bike miles		
strength time		
total		

soreness _____

notes _____

_____

_____

_____

_____

_____

Period: _____   **Planned Hours:** _____

MONDAY _____/_____/_____

▨ sleep ▨ fatigue ▨ stress ▨ soreness

resting heart rate_____weight_____

planned workout_____

_____

_____

weather_____

route_____

_____

_____

_____

dist._____time_____

zone 1_____2_____3_____4_____5_____

avg. HR_____avg. power_____

workout rating_____

notes _____

_____

_____

_____

_____

_____

_____

_____

_____

nutrition _____

_____

_____

_____

_____

TUESDAY _____/_____/_____

▨ sleep ▨ fatigue ▨ stress ▨ soreness

resting heart rate_____weight_____

planned workout_____

_____

_____

weather_____

route_____

_____

_____

_____

dist._____time_____

zone 1_____2_____3_____4_____5_____

avg. HR_____avg. power_____

workout rating_____

notes _____

_____

_____

_____

_____

_____

_____

_____

_____

nutrition _____

_____

_____

_____

_____

week goals: ■ _____
■ _____
■ _____

WEDNESDAY___/___/___

■ sleep ■ fatigue ■ stress ■ soreness

resting heart rate_____weight_____

planned workout_____

_____

_____

weather_____

route_____

_____

_____

_____

dist._____time_____

zone 1_____2_____3_____4_____5_____

avg. HR_____avg. power_____

workout rating_____

notes _____

_____

_____

_____

_____

_____

_____

_____

_____

_____

nutrition _____

_____

_____

_____

THURSDAY___/___/___

■ sleep ■ fatigue ■ stress ■ soreness

resting heart rate_____weight_____

planned workout_____

_____

_____

weather_____

route_____

_____

_____

_____

dist._____time_____

zone 1_____2_____3_____4_____5_____

avg. HR_____avg. power_____

workout rating_____

notes _____

_____

_____

_____

_____

_____

_____

_____

_____

_____

nutrition _____

_____

_____

_____

FRIDAY _____ / _____ / _____

☐ sleep ☐ fatigue ☐ stress ☐ soreness

resting heart rate_____weight_____

planned workout_____

_____

_____

weather_____

route_____

_____

_____

_____

_____

dist._____time_____

zone 1_____2_____3_____4_____5_____

avg. HR_____avg. power_____

workout rating_____

notes _____

_____

_____

_____

_____

_____

_____

_____

_____

_____

nutrition _____

_____

_____

_____

SATURDAY _____ / _____ / _____

☐ sleep ☐ fatigue ☐ stress ☐ soreness

resting heart rate_____weight_____

planned workout_____

_____

weather_____

route_____

_____

_____

_____

_____

dist._____time_____

zone 1_____2_____3_____4_____5_____

avg. HR_____avg. power_____

workout rating_____

notes _____

_____

_____

_____

_____

_____

_____

_____

_____

nutrition _____

_____

_____

_____

_____

SUNDAY _____/_____/_____

■ sleep ■ fatigue ■ stress ■ soreness

resting heart rate_____weight_____

planned workout_____

_____

_____

weather_____

route_____

_____

_____

_____

_____

dist._____time_____

zone 1_____2_____3_____4_____5_____

avg. HR_____avg. power_____

workout rating_____

notes _____

_____

_____

_____

_____

_____

_____

_____

_____

nutrition _____

_____

_____

_____

RACING

race 1 _____

category_____

distance_____time _____

result _____upgrade pts. _____

notes _____

_____

_____

_____

race 2 _____

category_____

distance_____time _____

result _____upgrade pts. _____

notes _____

_____

_____

WEEKLY SUMMARY

	weekly total	YTD
bike time		
bike miles		
strength time		
total		

soreness _____

notes _____

_____

_____

_____

_____

_____

_____

Period: _____   **Planned Hours:** _____

MONDAY _____/_____/_____

☐ sleep ☐ fatigue ☐ stress ☐ soreness

resting heart rate_____weight_____

planned workout_____

_____

_____

weather_____

route_____

_____

_____

_____

dist._____time_____

zone 1_____2_____3_____4_____5_____

avg. HR_____avg. power_____

workout rating_____

notes _____

_____

_____

_____

_____

_____

_____

_____

_____

nutrition _____

_____

_____

_____

_____

TUESDAY _____/_____/_____

☐ sleep ☐ fatigue ☐ stress ☐ soreness

resting heart rate_____weight_____

planned workout_____

_____

_____

weather_____

route_____

_____

_____

_____

dist._____time_____

zone 1_____2_____3_____4_____5_____

avg. HR_____avg. power_____

workout rating_____

notes _____

_____

_____

_____

_____

_____

_____

_____

_____

nutrition _____

_____

_____

_____

_____

week goals: ■ _____
■ _____
■ _____

WEDNESDAY____/____/____

■ sleep ■ fatigue ■ stress ■ soreness

resting heart rate_____weight_____

planned workout_____
_____
_____

weather_____

route_____
_____
_____
_____

dist._____time_____

zone 1_____2_____3_____4_____5_____

avg. HR_____avg. power_____

workout rating_____

notes _____
_____
_____
_____
_____
_____
_____
_____
_____
_____
_____
_____

nutrition _____
_____
_____
_____
_____

THURSDAY_____/_____/_____

■ sleep ■ fatigue ■ stress ■ soreness

resting heart rate_____weight_____

planned workout_____
_____
_____

weather_____

route_____
_____
_____
_____

dist._____time_____

zone 1_____2_____3_____4_____5_____

avg. HR_____avg. power_____

workout rating_____

notes _____
_____
_____
_____
_____
_____
_____
_____
_____
_____

nutrition _____
_____
_____

FRIDAY_____/_____/_____

▢ sleep ▢ fatigue ▢ stress ▢ soreness

resting heart rate_____weight_____

planned workout_____

_____

_____

weather_____

route_____

_____

_____

_____

_____

dist._____time_____

zone 1_____2_____3_____4_____5_____

avg. HR_____avg. power_____

workout rating_____

notes _____

_____

_____

_____

_____

_____

_____

_____

_____

_____

_____

nutrition _____

_____

_____

_____

SATURDAY_____/_____/_____

▢ sleep ▢ fatigue ▢ stress ▢ soreness

resting heart rate_____weight_____

planned workout_____

_____

_____

weather_____

route_____

_____

_____

_____

_____

dist._____time_____

zone 1_____2_____3_____4_____5_____

avg. HR_____avg. power_____

workout rating_____

notes _____

_____

_____

_____

_____

_____

_____

_____

_____

_____

_____

nutrition _____

_____

_____

_____

SUNDAY _____/_____/_____

■ sleep ■ fatigue ■ stress ■ soreness

resting heart rate_____weight_____

planned workout_____

_____

_____

weather_____

route_____

_____

_____

_____

dist._____time_____

zone 1_____2_____3_____4_____5_____

avg. HR_____avg. power_____

workout rating_____

notes _____

_____

_____

_____

_____

_____

_____

_____

_____

nutrition _____

_____

_____

_____

_____

RACING

race 1 _____

category_____

distance_____time _____

result _____upgrade pts. _____

notes _____

_____

_____

_____

race 2 _____

category_____

distance_____time _____

result _____upgrade pts. _____

notes _____

_____

_____

WEEKLY SUMMARY

	weekly total	YTD
bike time		
bike miles		
strength time		
total		

soreness _____

notes _____

_____

_____

_____

_____

_____

Period: _____   **Planned Hours:** _____

MONDAY _____/_____/_____

☐ sleep ☐ fatigue ☐ stress ☐ soreness

resting heart rate_____weight_____

planned workout_____

_____

_____

weather_____

route_____

_____

_____

_____

dist._____time_____

zone 1_____2_____3_____4_____5_____

avg. HR_____avg. power_____

workout rating_____

notes _____

_____

_____

_____

_____

_____

_____

_____

_____

nutrition _____

_____

_____

_____

_____

TUESDAY_____/_____/_____

☐ sleep ☐ fatigue ☐ stress ☐ soreness

resting heart rate_____weight_____

planned workout_____

_____

_____

weather_____

route_____

_____

_____

_____

dist._____time_____

zone 1_____2_____3_____4_____5_____

avg. HR_____avg. power_____

workout rating_____

notes _____

_____

_____

_____

_____

_____

_____

_____

_____

nutrition _____

_____

_____

_____

week goals: ▪ _____
▪ _____
▪ _____

WEDNESDAY___/___/___

▪ sleep ▪ fatigue ▪ stress ▪ soreness

resting heart rate_____weight_____

planned workout_____

_____

_____

weather_____

route_____

_____

_____

_____

dist._____time_____

zone 1_____2_____3_____4_____5_____

avg. HR_____avg. power_____

workout rating_____

notes _____

_____

_____

_____

_____

_____

_____

_____

nutrition _____

_____

_____

_____

THURSDAY___/___/___

▪ sleep ▪ fatigue ▪ stress ▪ soreness

resting heart rate_____weight_____

planned workout_____

_____

_____

weather_____

route_____

_____

_____

_____

dist._____time_____

zone 1_____2_____3_____4_____5_____

avg. HR_____avg. power_____

workout rating_____

notes _____

_____

_____

_____

_____

_____

_____

_____

nutrition _____

_____

_____

_____

FRIDAY _____/_____/_____

▪ sleep ▪ fatigue ▪ stress ▪ soreness

resting heart rate_____weight_____

planned workout_____

_____

_____

weather_____

route_____

_____

_____

_____

_____

dist._____time_____

zone 1_____2_____3_____4_____5_____

avg. HR_____avg. power_____

workout rating_____

notes _____

_____

_____

_____

_____

_____

_____

_____

_____

_____

_____

nutrition _____

_____

_____

_____

SATURDAY_____/_____/_____

▪ sleep ▪ fatigue ▪ stress ▪ soreness

resting heart rate_____weight_____

planned workout_____

_____

_____

weather_____

route_____

_____

_____

_____

_____

dist._____time_____

zone 1_____2_____3_____4_____5_____

avg. HR_____avg. power_____

workout rating_____

notes _____

_____

_____

_____

_____

_____

_____

_____

_____

_____

_____

nutrition _____

_____

_____

_____

SUNDAY _____/_____/_____

■ sleep ■ fatigue ■ stress ■ soreness

resting heart rate_____weight_____

planned workout_____

_____

_____

weather_____

route_____

_____

_____

_____

_____

dist._____time_____

zone 1_____2_____3_____4_____5_____

avg. HR_____avg. power_____

workout rating_____

notes _____

_____

_____

_____

_____

_____

_____

_____

_____

_____

_____

_____

nutrition _____

_____

_____

_____

_____

RACING

race 1 _____

category_____

distance_____time _____

result _____upgrade pts. _____

notes _____

_____

_____

_____

race 2 _____

category_____

distance_____time _____

result _____upgrade pts. _____

notes _____

_____

_____

WEEKLY SUMMARY

	weekly total	YTD
bike time		
bike miles		
strength time		
total		

soreness _____

notes _____

_____

_____

_____

_____

_____

Period: _____   **Planned Hours:** _____

MONDAY _____/_____/_____

☐ sleep ☐ fatigue ☐ stress ☐ soreness

resting heart rate_____weight_____

planned workout_____

_____

_____

weather_____

route_____

_____

_____

_____

dist._____time_____

zone 1_____2_____3_____4_____5_____

avg. HR_____avg. power_____

workout rating_____

notes _____

_____

_____

_____

_____

_____

_____

_____

_____

nutrition _____

_____

_____

_____

TUESDAY _____/_____/_____

☐ sleep ☐ fatigue ☐ stress ☐ soreness

resting heart rate_____weight_____

planned workout_____

_____

_____

weather_____

route_____

_____

_____

_____

dist._____time_____

zone 1_____2_____3_____4_____5_____

avg. HR_____avg. power_____

workout rating_____

notes _____

_____

_____

_____

_____

_____

_____

_____

_____

nutrition _____

_____

_____

_____

week goals: ■ _____
■ _____
■ _____

WEDNESDAY____/____/____

■ sleep ■ fatigue ■ stress ■ soreness

resting heart rate_____weight_____

planned workout_____
_____
_____

weather_____

route_____
_____
_____
_____

dist._____time_____

zone 1_____2_____3_____4_____5_____

avg. HR_____avg. power_____

workout rating_____

notes _____
_____
_____
_____
_____
_____
_____
_____
_____
_____

nutrition _____
_____
_____
_____
_____

THURSDAY_____/_____/_____

■ sleep ■ fatigue ■ stress ■ soreness

resting heart rate_____weight_____

planned workout_____
_____
_____

weather_____

route_____
_____
_____
_____

dist._____time_____

zone 1_____2_____3_____4_____5_____

avg. HR_____avg. power_____

workout rating_____

notes _____
_____
_____
_____
_____
_____
_____
_____
_____
_____

nutrition _____
_____
_____
_____
_____

FRIDAY _____/_____/_____

☐ sleep ☐ fatigue ☐ stress ☐ soreness

resting heart rate_____weight_____

planned workout_____

_____

_____

weather_____

route_____

_____

_____

_____

_____

dist._____time_____

zone 1_____2_____3_____4_____5_____

avg. HR_____avg. power_____

workout rating_____

notes _____

_____

_____

_____

_____

_____

_____

_____

_____

nutrition _____

_____

_____

_____

SATURDAY _____/_____/_____

☐ sleep ☐ fatigue ☐ stress ☐ soreness

resting heart rate_____weight_____

planned workout_____

_____

_____

weather_____

route_____

_____

_____

_____

_____

_____

dist._____time_____

zone 1_____2_____3_____4_____5_____

avg. HR_____avg. power_____

workout rating_____

notes _____

_____

_____

_____

_____

_____

_____

_____

_____

nutrition _____

_____

_____

_____

SUNDAY _____/_____/_____

■ sleep ■ fatigue ■ stress ■ soreness

resting heart rate_____weight_____

planned workout_____
_____
_____

weather_____

route_____
_____
_____
_____

dist._____time_____

zone 1_____2_____3_____4_____5_____

avg. HR_____avg. power_____

workout rating_____

notes _____
_____
_____
_____
_____
_____
_____
_____
_____

nutrition _____
_____
_____
_____
_____

RACING

race 1 _____

category_____

distance_____time _____

result _____upgrade pts. _____

notes _____
_____
_____
_____

race 2 _____

category_____

distance_____time _____

result _____upgrade pts. _____

notes _____
_____
_____

WEEKLY SUMMARY

	weekly total	YTD
bike time		
bike miles		
strength time		
total		

soreness _____

notes _____
_____
_____
_____
_____
_____
_____

Period: _____

Planned Hours: _____

MONDAY _____/_____/_____

☐ sleep ☐ fatigue ☐ stress ☐ soreness

resting heart rate_____weight_____

planned workout_____

_____

_____

weather_____

route_____

_____

_____

_____

dist._____time_____

zone 1_____2_____3_____4_____5_____

avg. HR_____avg. power_____

workout rating_____

notes _____

_____

_____

_____

_____

_____

_____

_____

nutrition _____

_____

_____

_____

TUESDAY _____/_____/_____

☐ sleep ☐ fatigue ☐ stress ☐ soreness

resting heart rate_____weight_____

planned workout_____

_____

_____

weather_____

route_____

_____

_____

_____

dist._____time_____

zone 1_____2_____3_____4_____5_____

avg. HR_____avg. power_____

workout rating_____

notes _____

_____

_____

_____

_____

_____

_____

_____

nutrition _____

_____

_____

_____

week goals: ■ _____
■ _____
■ _____

WEDNESDAY___/___/___

■ sleep ■ fatigue ■ stress ■ soreness

resting heart rate_____weight_____

planned workout_____
_____
_____

weather_____

route_____
_____
_____
_____

dist._____time_____

zone 1_____2_____3_____4_____5_____

avg. HR_____avg. power_____

workout rating_____

notes _____
_____
_____
_____
_____
_____
_____

nutrition _____
_____
_____
_____
_____

THURSDAY___/___/___

■ sleep ■ fatigue ■ stress ■ soreness

resting heart rate_____weight_____

planned workout_____
_____
_____

weather_____

route_____
_____
_____
_____

dist._____time_____

zone 1_____2_____3_____4_____5_____

avg. HR_____avg. power_____

workout rating_____

notes _____
_____
_____
_____
_____
_____
_____

nutrition _____
_____
_____
_____
_____

FRIDAY _____/_____/_____

◼ sleep ◼ fatigue ◼ stress ◼ soreness

resting heart rate_____weight_____

planned workout_____

_____

_____

weather_____

route_____

_____

_____

_____

_____

dist._____time_____

zone 1_____2_____3_____4_____5_____

avg. HR_____avg. power_____

workout rating_____

notes _____

_____

_____

_____

_____

_____

_____

_____

_____

_____

nutrition _____

_____

_____

_____

_____

SATURDAY_____/_____/_____

◼ sleep ◼ fatigue ◼ stress ◼ soreness

resting heart rate_____weight_____

planned workout_____

_____

_____

weather_____

route_____

_____

_____

_____

_____

dist._____time_____

zone 1_____2_____3_____4_____5_____

avg. HR_____avg. power_____

workout rating_____

notes _____

_____

_____

_____

_____

_____

_____

_____

_____

_____

nutrition _____

_____

_____

_____

_____

SUNDAY _____/_____/_____

☐ sleep ☐ fatigue ☐ stress ☐ soreness

resting heart rate_____weight_____

planned workout_____

_____

_____

weather_____

route_____

_____

_____

_____

_____

dist._____time_____

zone 1_____2_____3_____4_____5_____

avg. HR_____avg. power_____

workout rating_____

notes _____

_____

_____

_____

_____

_____

_____

_____

_____

nutrition _____

_____

_____

_____

RACING

race 1 _____

category _____

distance_____time _____

result _____upgrade pts. _____

notes _____

_____

_____

_____

race 2 _____

category _____

distance_____time _____

result _____upgrade pts. _____

notes _____

_____

_____

_____

WEEKLY SUMMARY

	weekly total	YTD
bike time		
bike miles		
strength time		
total		

soreness _____

notes _____

_____

_____

_____

_____

_____

_____

Period: _____   **Planned Hours:** _____

MONDAY _____/_____/_____

▪ sleep ▪ fatigue ▪ stress ▪ soreness

resting heart rate_____weight_____

planned workout_____

_____

_____

weather_____

route_____

_____

_____

_____

dist._____time_____

zone 1_____2_____3_____4_____5_____

avg. HR_____avg. power_____

workout rating_____

notes _____
_____
_____
_____
_____
_____
_____
_____

nutrition _____
_____
_____
_____
_____

TUESDAY_____/_____/_____

▪ sleep ▪ fatigue ▪ stress ▪ soreness

resting heart rate_____weight_____

planned workout_____

_____

_____

weather_____

route_____

_____

_____

_____

dist._____time_____

zone 1_____2_____3_____4_____5_____

avg. HR_____avg. power_____

workout rating_____

notes _____
_____
_____
_____
_____
_____
_____
_____

nutrition _____
_____
_____
_____
_____

week goals: ▪ _____
▪ _____
▪ _____

WEDNESDAY____/____/____

▪ sleep ▪ fatigue ▪ stress ▪ soreness

resting heart rate_____weight_____

planned workout_____
_____
_____

weather_____

route_____
_____
_____

dist._____time_____

zone 1_____2_____3_____4_____5_____

avg. HR_____avg. power_____

workout rating_____

notes _____
_____
_____
_____
_____
_____
_____
_____
_____

nutrition _____
_____
_____
_____
_____

THURSDAY____/____/____

▪ sleep ▪ fatigue ▪ stress ▪ soreness

resting heart rate_____weight_____

planned workout_____
_____
_____

weather_____

route_____
_____
_____

dist._____time_____

zone 1_____2_____3_____4_____5_____

avg. HR_____avg. power_____

workout rating_____

notes _____
_____
_____
_____
_____
_____
_____
_____

nutrition _____
_____
_____
_____

FRIDAY _____/_____/_____

☐ sleep ☐ fatigue ☐ stress ☐ soreness

resting heart rate_____weight_____

planned workout_____

_____

_____

weather_____

route_____

_____

_____

_____

_____

dist._____time_____

zone 1_____2_____3_____4_____5_____

avg. HR_____avg. power_____

workout rating_____

notes _____

_____

_____

_____

_____

_____

_____

_____

nutrition _____

_____

_____

_____

_____

SATURDAY_____/_____/_____

☐ sleep ☐ fatigue ☐ stress ☐ soreness

resting heart rate_____weight_____

planned workout_____

_____

_____

weather_____

route_____

_____

_____

_____

_____

dist._____time_____

zone 1_____2_____3_____4_____5_____

avg. HR_____avg. power_____

workout rating_____

notes _____

_____

_____

_____

_____

_____

_____

_____

nutrition _____

_____

_____

_____

_____

SUNDAY_____/_____/_____

■ sleep ■ fatigue ■ stress ■ soreness

resting heart rate_____weight_____

planned workout_____

_____

_____

weather_____

route_____

_____

_____

_____

_____

dist._____time_____

zone 1_____2_____3_____4_____5_____

avg. HR_____avg. power_____

workout rating_____

notes _____

_____

_____

_____

_____

_____

_____

_____

_____

_____

nutrition _____

_____

_____

_____

_____

RACING

race 1 _____

category_____

distance_____time _____

result _____upgrade pts. _____

notes _____

_____

_____

_____

race 2 _____

category_____

distance_____time _____

result _____upgrade pts. _____

notes _____

_____

_____

WEEKLY SUMMARY

	weekly total	YTD
bike time		
bike miles		
strength time		
total		

soreness_____

notes _____

_____

_____

_____

_____

_____

Period: _____

Planned Hours: _____

MONDAY _____/_____/_____

sleep ▪ fatigue ▪ stress ▪ soreness

resting heart rate_____weight_____

planned workout_____

_____

_____

weather_____

route_____

_____

_____

_____

dist._____time_____

zone 1_____2_____3_____4_____5_____

avg. HR_____avg. power_____

workout rating_____

notes _____

_____

_____

_____

_____

_____

_____

_____

_____

nutrition _____

_____

_____

_____

TUESDAY_____/_____/_____

sleep ▪ fatigue ▪ stress ▪ soreness

resting heart rate_____weight_____

planned workout_____

_____

_____

weather_____

route_____

_____

_____

_____

dist._____time_____

zone 1_____2_____3_____4_____5_____

avg. HR_____avg. power_____

workout rating_____

notes _____

_____

_____

_____

_____

_____

_____

_____

_____

nutrition _____

_____

_____

_____

week goals: ▪ _____
▪ _____
▪ _____

WEDNESDAY____/____/____

▪ sleep ▪ fatigue ▪ stress ▪ soreness

resting heart rate_____weight_____

planned workout_____

_____

_____

weather_____

route_____

_____

_____

_____

dist._____time_____

zone 1_____2_____3_____4_____5_____

avg. HR_____avg. power_____

workout rating_____

notes _____

_____

_____

_____

_____

_____

_____

_____

_____

nutrition _____

_____

_____

_____

THURSDAY_____/_____/_____

▪ sleep ▪ fatigue ▪ stress ▪ soreness

resting heart rate_____weight_____

planned workout_____

_____

weather_____

route_____

_____

_____

_____

dist._____time_____

zone 1_____2_____3_____4_____5_____

avg. HR_____avg. power_____

workout rating_____

notes _____

_____

_____

_____

_____

_____

_____

_____

nutrition _____

_____

_____

_____

FRIDAY _____/_____/_____

☐ sleep ☐ fatigue ☐ stress ☐ soreness

resting heart rate_____weight_____

planned workout_____

_____

_____

weather_____

route_____

_____

_____

_____

_____

dist._____time_____

zone 1_____2_____3_____4_____5_____

avg. HR_____avg. power_____

workout rating_____

notes _____

_____

_____

_____

_____

_____

_____

_____

_____

_____

_____

nutrition _____

_____

_____

_____

_____

SATURDAY _____/_____/_____

☐ sleep ☐ fatigue ☐ stress ☐ soreness

resting heart rate_____weight_____

planned workout_____

_____

_____

weather_____

route_____

_____

_____

_____

_____

dist._____time_____

zone 1_____2_____3_____4_____5_____

avg. HR_____avg. power_____

workout rating_____

notes _____

_____

_____

_____

_____

_____

_____

_____

_____

nutrition _____

_____

_____

_____

SUNDAY _____/_____/_____

■ sleep ■ fatigue ■ stress ■ soreness

resting heart rate_____weight_____

planned workout_____

_____

_____

weather_____

route_____

_____

_____

_____

_____

dist._____time_____

zone 1_____2_____3_____4_____5_____

avg. HR_____avg. power_____

workout rating_____

notes _____

_____

_____

_____

_____

_____

_____

_____

_____

nutrition _____

_____

_____

_____

_____

RACING

race 1 _____

category_____

distance_____time _____

result _____upgrade pts. _____

notes _____

_____

_____

_____

race 2 _____

category_____

distance_____time _____

result _____upgrade pts. _____

notes _____

_____

_____

WEEKLY SUMMARY

	weekly total	YTD
bike time		
bike miles		
strength time		
total		

soreness _____

notes _____

_____

_____

_____

_____

_____

Period: _____ **Planned Hours:** _____

MONDAY _____/_____/_____

☐ sleep ☐ fatigue ☐ stress ☐ soreness

resting heart rate_____weight_____

planned workout_____

_____

_____

weather_____

route_____

_____

_____

_____

dist._____time_____

zone 1_____2_____3_____4_____5_____

avg. HR_____avg. power_____

workout rating_____

notes _____

_____

_____

_____

_____

_____

_____

_____

_____

nutrition _____

_____

_____

_____

_____

TUESDAY_____/_____/_____

☐ sleep ☐ fatigue ☐ stress ☐ soreness

resting heart rate_____weight_____

planned workout_____

_____

_____

weather_____

route_____

_____

_____

_____

dist._____time_____

zone 1_____2_____3_____4_____5_____

avg. HR_____avg. power_____

workout rating_____

notes _____

_____

_____

_____

_____

_____

_____

_____

nutrition _____

_____

_____

_____

_____

week goals: _____
■ _____
■ _____

WEDNESDAY____/____/____

■ sleep ■ fatigue ■ stress ■ soreness

resting heart rate_____weight_____

planned workout_____

_____

_____

weather_____

route_____

_____

_____

_____

dist._____time_____

zone 1_____2_____3_____4_____5_____

avg. HR_____avg. power_____

workout rating_____

notes _____

_____

_____

_____

_____

_____

_____

_____

nutrition _____

_____

_____

_____

_____

THURSDAY_____/_____/_____

■ sleep ■ fatigue ■ stress ■ soreness

resting heart rate_____weight_____

planned workout_____

_____

weather_____

route_____

_____

_____

_____

dist._____time_____

zone 1_____2_____3_____4_____5_____

avg. HR_____avg. power_____

workout rating_____

notes _____

_____

_____

_____

_____

_____

_____

_____

nutrition _____

_____

_____

_____

_____

FRIDAY _____/_____/_____

■ sleep ■ fatigue ■ stress ■ soreness

resting heart rate_____weight_____

planned workout_____

_____

_____

weather_____

route_____

_____

_____

_____

_____

dist._____time_____

zone 1_____2_____3_____4_____5_____

avg. HR_____avg. power_____

workout rating_____

notes _____

_____

_____

_____

_____

_____

_____

_____

_____

_____

nutrition _____

_____

_____

_____

SATURDAY_____/_____/_____

■ sleep ■ fatigue ■ stress ■ soreness

resting heart rate_____weight_____

planned workout_____

_____

_____

weather_____

route_____

_____

_____

_____

_____

dist._____time_____

zone 1_____2_____3_____4_____5_____

avg. HR_____avg. power_____

workout rating_____

notes _____

_____

_____

_____

_____

_____

_____

_____

_____

_____

nutrition _____

_____

_____

_____

SUNDAY _____/_____/_____

◻ sleep ◻ fatigue ◻ stress ◻ soreness

resting heart rate_____weight_____

planned workout_____

_____

_____

weather_____

route_____

_____

_____

_____

_____

dist._____time_____

zone 1_____2_____3_____4_____5_____

avg. HR_____avg. power_____

workout rating_____

notes _____

_____

_____

_____

_____

_____

_____

_____

_____

_____

_____

_____

nutrition _____

_____

_____

_____

_____

RACING

race 1 _____

category_____

distance_____time _____

result _____upgrade pts. _____

notes _____

_____

_____

_____

race 2 _____

category_____

distance_____time _____

result _____upgrade pts. _____

notes _____

_____

_____

WEEKLY SUMMARY

	weekly total	YTD
bike time		
bike miles		
strength time		
total		

soreness _____

notes _____

_____

_____

_____

_____

_____

_____

_____

Period: _____   **Planned Hours:** _____

MONDAY _____/_____/_____

■ sleep   ■ fatigue   ■ stress   ■ soreness

resting heart rate_____weight_____

planned workout_____

_____

_____

weather_____

route_____

_____

_____

_____

dist._____time_____

zone 1_____2_____3_____4_____5_____

avg. HR_____avg. power_____

workout rating_____

notes _____

_____

_____

_____

_____

_____

_____

_____

nutrition _____

_____

_____

_____

_____

TUESDAY_____/_____/_____

■ sleep   ■ fatigue   ■ stress   ■ soreness

resting heart rate_____weight_____

planned workout_____

_____

_____

weather_____

route_____

_____

_____

_____

dist._____time_____

zone 1_____2_____3_____4_____5_____

avg. HR_____avg. power_____

workout rating_____

notes _____

_____

_____

_____

_____

_____

_____

_____

nutrition _____

_____

_____

_____

_____

week goals: ■ _____
■ _____
■ _____

WEDNESDAY____/____/____

■ sleep ■ fatigue ■ stress ■ soreness

resting heart rate_____weight_____

planned workout_____

_____

_____

weather_____

route_____

_____

_____

_____

dist._____time_____

zone 1_____2_____3_____4_____5_____

avg. HR_____avg. power_____

workout rating_____

notes _____

_____

_____

_____

_____

_____

_____

_____

_____

_____

nutrition _____

_____

_____

_____

_____

THURSDAY____/____/____

■ sleep ■ fatigue ■ stress ■ soreness

resting heart rate_____weight_____

planned workout_____

_____

_____

weather_____

route_____

_____

_____

_____

dist._____time_____

zone 1_____2_____3_____4_____5_____

avg. HR_____avg. power_____

workout rating_____

notes _____

_____

_____

_____

_____

_____

_____

_____

_____

_____

nutrition _____

_____

_____

_____

_____

FRIDAY _____/_____/_____

☐ sleep ☐ fatigue ☐ stress ☐ soreness

resting heart rate_____weight_____

planned workout_____

_____

_____

weather_____

route_____

_____

_____

_____

_____

dist._____time_____

zone 1_____2_____3_____4_____5_____

avg. HR_____avg. power_____

workout rating_____

notes _____

_____

_____

_____

_____

_____

_____

_____

nutrition _____

_____

_____

_____

_____

SATURDAY _____/_____/_____

☐ sleep ☐ fatigue ☐ stress ☐ soreness

resting heart rate_____weight_____

planned workout_____

_____

weather_____

route_____

_____

_____

_____

_____

dist._____time_____

zone 1_____2_____3_____4_____5_____

avg. HR_____avg. power_____

workout rating_____

notes _____

_____

_____

_____

_____

_____

_____

_____

nutrition _____

_____

_____

_____

SUNDAY _____/_____/_____

■ sleep ■ fatigue ■ stress ■ soreness

resting heart rate_____weight_____

planned workout_____

_____

_____

weather_____

route_____

_____

_____

_____

_____

dist._____time_____

zone 1_____2_____3_____4_____5_____

avg. HR_____avg. power_____

workout rating_____

notes _____

_____

_____

_____

_____

_____

_____

_____

_____

_____

nutrition _____

_____

_____

_____

RACING

race 1 _____

category_____

distance_____time _____

result _____upgrade pts. _____

notes _____

_____

_____

_____

race 2 _____

category_____

distance_____time _____

result _____upgrade pts. _____

notes _____

_____

_____

WEEKLY SUMMARY

	weekly total	YTD
bike time		
bike miles		
strength time		
total		

soreness _____

notes _____

_____

_____

_____

_____

_____

_____

Period: _____   **Planned Hours:** _____

MONDAY _____/_____/_____

☐ sleep ☐ fatigue ☐ stress ☐ soreness

resting heart rate_____weight_____

planned workout_____

_____

_____

weather_____

route_____

_____

_____

_____

dist._____time_____

zone 1_____2_____3_____4_____5_____

avg. HR_____avg. power_____

workout rating_____

notes _____

_____

_____

_____

_____

_____

_____

_____

_____

_____

_____

nutrition _____

_____

_____

_____

_____

TUESDAY_____/_____/_____

☐ sleep ☐ fatigue ☐ stress ☐ soreness

resting heart rate_____weight_____

planned workout_____

_____

_____

weather_____

route_____

_____

_____

_____

dist._____time_____

zone 1_____2_____3_____4_____5_____

avg. HR_____avg. power_____

workout rating_____

notes _____

_____

_____

_____

_____

_____

_____

_____

_____

_____

_____

nutrition _____

_____

_____

_____

_____

week goals: ■ _____
■ _____
■ _____

WEDNESDAY____/____/____

■ sleep ■ fatigue ■ stress ■ soreness

resting heart rate_____weight_____

planned workout_____

_____

_____

weather_____

route_____

_____

_____

_____

dist._____time_____

zone 1_____2_____3_____4_____5_____

avg. HR_____avg. power_____

workout rating_____

notes _____

_____

_____

_____

_____

_____

_____

_____

nutrition _____

_____

_____

_____

THURSDAY____/____/____

■ sleep ■ fatigue ■ stress ■ soreness

resting heart rate_____weight_____

planned workout_____

_____

_____

weather_____

route_____

_____

_____

_____

dist._____time_____

zone 1_____2_____3_____4_____5_____

avg. HR_____avg. power_____

workout rating_____

notes _____

_____

_____

_____

_____

_____

_____

_____

nutrition _____

_____

_____

_____

FRIDAY _____/_____/_____

sleep ▦ fatigue ▦ stress ▦ soreness

resting heart rate_____weight_____

planned workout_____

_____

_____

weather_____

route_____

_____

_____

_____

_____

dist._____time_____

zone 1_____2_____3_____4_____5_____

avg. HR_____avg. power_____

workout rating_____

notes _____

_____

_____

_____

_____

_____

_____

_____

_____

nutrition _____

_____

_____

_____

_____

SATURDAY_____/_____/_____

sleep ▦ fatigue ▦ stress ▦ soreness

resting heart rate_____weight_____

planned workout_____

_____

weather_____

route_____

_____

_____

_____

_____

dist._____time_____

zone 1_____2_____3_____4_____5_____

avg. HR_____avg. power_____

workout rating_____

notes _____

_____

_____

_____

_____

_____

_____

_____

_____

nutrition _____

_____

_____

_____

SUNDAY _____/_____/_____

 ▨ sleep ▨ fatigue ▨ stress ▨ soreness

resting heart rate_____weight_____

planned workout_____

_____

_____

weather_____

route_____

_____

_____

_____

dist._____time_____

zone 1_____2_____3_____4_____5_____

avg. HR_____avg. power_____

workout rating_____

notes _____

_____

_____

_____

_____

_____

_____

_____

_____

_____

_____

nutrition _____

_____

_____

_____

_____

RACING

race 1 _____

category_____

distance_____time_____

result _____upgrade pts. _____

notes _____

_____

_____

_____

race 2 _____

category_____

distance_____time_____

result _____upgrade pts. _____

notes _____

_____

_____

WEEKLY SUMMARY

	weekly total	YTD
bike time		
bike miles		
strength time		
total		

soreness _____

notes _____

_____

_____

_____

_____

_____

_____

_____

_____

Period: _____ **Planned Hours:** _____

MONDAY _____/_____/_____

■ sleep ■ fatigue ■ stress ■ soreness

resting heart rate_____weight_____

planned workout_____

_____

_____

weather_____

route_____

_____

_____

dist._____time_____

zone 1_____2_____3_____4_____5_____

avg. HR_____avg. power_____

workout rating_____

notes _____

_____

_____

_____

_____

_____

_____

_____

_____

nutrition _____

_____

_____

_____

_____

TUESDAY_____/_____/_____

■ sleep ■ fatigue ■ stress ■ soreness

resting heart rate_____weight_____

planned workout_____

_____

_____

weather_____

route_____

_____

_____

dist._____time_____

zone 1_____2_____3_____4_____5_____

avg. HR_____avg. power_____

workout rating_____

notes _____

_____

_____

_____

_____

_____

_____

_____

_____

nutrition _____

_____

_____

_____

week goals: ▪ _____
▪ _____
▪ _____

WEDNESDAY___/___/___

▪ sleep ▪ fatigue ▪ stress ▪ soreness

resting heart rate_____weight_____

planned workout_____
_____
_____

weather_____

route_____
_____
_____
_____

dist._____time_____

zone 1_____2_____3_____4_____5_____

avg. HR_____avg. power_____

workout rating_____

notes _____
_____
_____
_____
_____
_____
_____
_____
_____

nutrition _____
_____
_____
_____

THURSDAY___/___/___

▪ sleep ▪ fatigue ▪ stress ▪ soreness

resting heart rate_____weight_____

planned workout_____
_____
_____

weather_____

route_____
_____
_____
_____

dist._____time_____

zone 1_____2_____3_____4_____5_____

avg. HR_____avg. power_____

workout rating_____

notes _____
_____
_____
_____
_____
_____
_____
_____
_____

nutrition _____
_____
_____
_____

FRIDAY _____/_____/_____

■ sleep   ■ fatigue   ■ stress   ■ soreness

resting heart rate_____weight_____

planned workout_____

_____

_____

weather_____

route_____

_____

_____

_____

_____

dist._____time_____

zone 1_____2_____3_____4_____5_____

avg. HR_____avg. power_____

workout rating_____

notes _____

_____

_____

_____

_____

_____

_____

_____

_____

nutrition _____

_____

_____

_____

_____

SATURDAY_____/_____/_____

■ sleep   ■ fatigue   ■ stress   ■ soreness

resting heart rate_____weight_____

planned workout_____

_____

_____

weather_____

route_____

_____

_____

_____

_____

dist._____time_____

zone 1_____2_____3_____4_____5_____

avg. HR_____avg. power_____

workout rating_____

notes _____

_____

_____

_____

_____

_____

_____

_____

_____

nutrition _____

_____

_____

_____

_____

SUNDAY_____/_____/_____

■ sleep ■ fatigue ■ stress ■ soreness

resting heart rate_____weight_____

planned workout_____

_____

_____

weather_____

route_____

_____

_____

_____

_____

dist._____time_____

zone 1_____2_____3_____4_____5_____

avg. HR_____avg. power_____

workout rating_____

notes _____

_____

_____

_____

_____

_____

_____

_____

_____

_____

_____

nutrition _____

_____

_____

_____

_____

RACING

race 1 _____

category_____

distance_____time _____

result _____upgrade pts. _____

notes _____

_____

_____

_____

race 2 _____

category_____

distance_____time _____

result _____upgrade pts. _____

notes _____

_____

_____

WEEKLY SUMMARY

	weekly total	YTD
bike time		
bike miles		
strength time		
total		

soreness_____

notes _____

_____

_____

_____

_____

_____

_____

Period: _____   **Planned Hours:** _____

MONDAY _____/_____/_____

■ sleep ■ fatigue ■ stress ■ soreness

resting heart rate_____weight_____

planned workout_____

_____

_____

weather_____

route_____

_____

_____

dist._____time_____

zone 1_____2_____3_____4_____5_____

avg. HR_____avg. power_____

workout rating_____

notes _____

_____

_____

_____

_____

_____

_____

_____

_____

_____

nutrition _____

_____

_____

_____

_____

TUESDAY_____/_____/_____

■ sleep ■ fatigue ■ stress ■ soreness

resting heart rate_____weight_____

planned workout_____

_____

_____

weather_____

route_____

_____

_____

dist._____time_____

zone 1_____2_____3_____4_____5_____

avg. HR_____avg. power_____

workout rating_____

notes _____

_____

_____

_____

_____

_____

_____

_____

_____

_____

nutrition _____

_____

_____

_____

_____

week goals: ■ _____

■ _____

■ _____

WEDNESDAY____/____/____

■ sleep ■ fatigue ■ stress ■ soreness

resting heart rate_____weight_____

planned workout_____

_____

_____

weather_____

route_____

_____

_____

_____

dist._____time_____

zone 1_____2_____3_____4_____5_____

avg. HR_____avg. power_____

workout rating_____

notes _____

_____

_____

_____

_____

_____

_____

_____

_____

_____

_____

nutrition _____

_____

_____

_____

_____

THURSDAY____/____/____

■ sleep ■ fatigue ■ stress ■ soreness

resting heart rate_____weight_____

planned workout_____

_____

_____

weather_____

route_____

_____

_____

_____

dist._____time_____

zone 1_____2_____3_____4_____5_____

avg. HR_____avg. power_____

workout rating_____

notes _____

_____

_____

_____

_____

_____

_____

_____

_____

nutrition _____

_____

_____

_____

FRIDAY_____/_____/_____

■ sleep ■ fatigue ■ stress ■ soreness

resting heart rate_____weight_____

planned workout_____

_____

_____

weather_____

route_____

_____

_____

_____

_____

dist._____time_____

zone 1_____2_____3_____4_____5_____

avg. HR_____avg. power_____

workout rating_____

notes _____

_____

_____

_____

_____

_____

_____

_____

_____

_____

nutrition _____

_____

_____

_____

SATURDAY_____/_____/_____

■ sleep ■ fatigue ■ stress ■ soreness

resting heart rate_____weight_____

planned workout_____

_____

_____

weather_____

route_____

_____

_____

_____

_____

dist._____time_____

zone 1_____2_____3_____4_____5_____

avg. HR_____avg. power_____

workout rating_____

notes _____

_____

_____

_____

_____

_____

_____

_____

_____

_____

nutrition _____

_____

_____

_____

SUNDAY _____/_____/_____

☐ sleep ☐ fatigue ☐ stress ☐ soreness

resting heart rate_____weight_____

planned workout_____

_____

_____

weather_____

route_____

_____

_____

_____

_____

dist._____time_____

zone 1_____2_____3_____4_____5_____

avg. HR_____avg. power_____

workout rating_____

notes _____

_____

_____

_____

_____

_____

_____

_____

_____

_____

nutrition _____

_____

_____

_____

_____

RACING

race 1 _____

category_____

distance_____time _____

result _____upgrade pts. _____

notes _____

_____

_____

_____

race 2 _____

category_____

distance_____time _____

result _____upgrade pts. _____

notes _____

_____

_____

WEEKLY SUMMARY

	weekly total	YTD
bike time		
bike miles		
strength time		
total		

soreness _____

notes _____

_____

_____

_____

_____

_____

_____

Period: _____ **Planned Hours:** _____

MONDAY _____/_____/_____

▢ sleep ▢ fatigue ▢ stress ▢ soreness

resting heart rate_____weight_____

planned workout_____

_____

_____

weather_____

route_____

_____

_____

_____

dist._____time_____

zone 1_____2_____3_____4_____5_____

avg. HR_____avg. power_____

workout rating_____

notes _____

_____

_____

_____

_____

_____

_____

_____

_____

nutrition _____

_____

_____

_____

_____

_____

TUESDAY_____/_____/_____

▢ sleep ▢ fatigue ▢ stress ▢ soreness

resting heart rate_____weight_____

planned workout_____

_____

_____

weather_____

route_____

_____

_____

_____

dist._____time_____

zone 1_____2_____3_____4_____5_____

avg. HR_____avg. power_____

workout rating_____

notes _____

_____

_____

_____

_____

_____

_____

_____

_____

nutrition _____

_____

_____

_____

_____

week goals: ■ _____

■ _____

■ _____

WEDNESDAY___/___/___   notes _____

■ sleep ■ fatigue ■ stress ■ soreness

resting heart rate_____weight_____

planned workout_____

_____

_____

weather_____

route_____

_____

_____

_____

dist._____time_____   **nutrition** _____

zone 1_____2_____3_____4_____5_____

avg. HR_____avg. power_____

workout rating_____

THURSDAY___/___/___   notes _____

■ sleep ■ fatigue ■ stress ■ soreness

resting heart rate_____weight_____

planned workout_____

_____

_____

weather_____

route_____

_____

_____

_____

dist._____time_____   **nutrition** _____

zone 1_____2_____3_____4_____5_____

avg. HR_____avg. power_____

workout rating_____

FRIDAY _____/_____/_____

☐ sleep ☐ fatigue ☐ stress ☐ soreness

resting heart rate_____weight_____

planned workout_____

_____

_____

weather_____

route_____

_____

_____

_____

_____

dist._____time_____

zone 1_____2_____3_____4_____5_____

avg. HR_____avg. power_____

workout rating_____

notes _____

_____

_____

_____

_____

_____

_____

_____

_____

nutrition _____

_____

_____

_____

_____

_____

SATURDAY_____/_____/_____

☐ sleep ☐ fatigue ☐ stress ☐ soreness

resting heart rate_____weight_____

planned workout_____

_____

_____

weather_____

route_____

_____

_____

_____

_____

dist._____time_____

zone 1_____2_____3_____4_____5_____

avg. HR_____avg. power_____

workout rating_____

notes _____

_____

_____

_____

_____

_____

_____

_____

_____

nutrition _____

_____

_____

_____

_____

_____

SUNDAY _____/_____/_____

■ sleep ■ fatigue ■ stress ■ soreness

resting heart rate_____weight_____

planned workout_____

_____

_____

weather_____

route_____

_____

_____

_____

_____

dist._____time_____

zone 1_____2_____3_____4_____5_____

avg. HR_____avg. power_____

workout rating_____

notes _____

_____

_____

_____

_____

_____

_____

_____

_____

_____

nutrition _____

_____

_____

_____

RACING

race 1 _____

category_____

distance_____time _____

result _____upgrade pts. _____

notes _____

_____

_____

_____

race 2 _____

category_____

distance_____time _____

result _____upgrade pts. _____

notes _____

_____

_____

WEEKLY SUMMARY

	weekly total	YTD
bike time		
bike miles		
strength time		
total		

soreness _____

notes _____

_____

_____

_____

_____

_____

_____

Period: _____

Planned Hours: _____

MONDAY _____/_____/_____

■ sleep ■ fatigue ■ stress ■ soreness

resting heart rate_____weight_____

planned workout_____

_____

_____

weather_____

route_____

_____

_____

_____

dist._____time_____

zone 1_____2_____3_____4_____5_____

avg. HR_____avg. power_____

workout rating_____

notes _____

_____

_____

_____

_____

_____

_____

_____

_____

nutrition _____

_____

_____

_____

_____

TUESDAY_____/_____/_____

■ sleep ■ fatigue ■ stress ■ soreness

resting heart rate_____weight_____

planned workout_____

_____

_____

weather_____

route_____

_____

_____

_____

dist._____time_____

zone 1_____2_____3_____4_____5_____

avg. HR_____avg. power_____

workout rating_____

notes _____

_____

_____

_____

_____

_____

_____

_____

_____

nutrition _____

_____

_____

_____

_____

week goals:
■ _____
■ _____
■ _____

WEDNESDAY___/___/___

■ sleep ■ fatigue ■ stress ■ soreness

resting heart rate_____weight_____

planned workout_____

_____

_____

weather_____

route_____

_____

_____

dist._____time_____

zone 1_____2_____3_____4_____5_____

avg. HR_____avg. power_____

workout rating_____

notes _____

_____

_____

_____

_____

_____

_____

_____

_____

nutrition _____

_____

_____

_____

THURSDAY___/___/___

■ sleep ■ fatigue ■ stress ■ soreness

resting heart rate_____weight_____

planned workout_____

_____

_____

weather_____

route_____

_____

_____

dist._____time_____

zone 1_____2_____3_____4_____5_____

avg. HR_____avg. power_____

workout rating_____

notes _____

_____

_____

_____

_____

_____

_____

_____

_____

nutrition _____

_____

_____

_____

FRIDAY _____/_____/_____

▢ sleep ▢ fatigue ▢ stress ▢ soreness

resting heart rate_____weight_____

planned workout_____

_____

_____

weather_____

route_____

_____

_____

_____

dist._____time_____

zone 1_____2_____3_____4_____5_____

avg. HR_____avg. power_____

workout rating_____

notes _____

_____

_____

_____

_____

_____

_____

_____

nutrition _____

_____

_____

_____

_____

SATURDAY _____/_____/_____

▢ sleep ▢ fatigue ▢ stress ▢ soreness

resting heart rate_____weight_____

planned workout_____

_____

_____

weather_____

route_____

_____

_____

_____

dist._____time_____

zone 1_____2_____3_____4_____5_____

avg. HR_____avg. power_____

workout rating_____

notes _____

_____

_____

_____

_____

_____

_____

_____

nutrition _____

_____

_____

_____

_____

SUNDAY _____/_____/_____

■ sleep   ■ fatigue   ■ stress   ■ soreness

resting heart rate_____weight_____

planned workout_____

_____

_____

weather_____

route_____

_____

_____

_____

_____

dist._____time_____

zone 1_____2_____3_____4_____5_____

avg. HR_____avg. power_____

workout rating_____

notes _____

_____

_____

_____

_____

_____

_____

_____

nutrition _____

_____

_____

_____

_____

RACING

race 1 _____

category_____

distance_____time _____

result _____upgrade pts. _____

notes _____

_____

_____

_____

race 2 _____

category_____

distance_____time _____

result _____upgrade pts. _____

notes _____

_____

_____

WEEKLY SUMMARY

	weekly total	YTD
bike time		
bike miles		
strength time		
total		

soreness _____

notes _____

_____

_____

_____

_____

_____

_____

_____

Period: _____   **Planned Hours:** _____

MONDAY _____/_____/_____

☐ sleep ☐ fatigue ☐ stress ☐ soreness

resting heart rate_____weight_____

planned workout_____

_____

_____

weather_____

route_____

_____

_____

dist._____time_____

zone 1_____2_____3_____4_____5_____

avg. HR_____avg. power_____

workout rating_____

notes _____

_____

_____

_____

_____

_____

_____

_____

nutrition _____

_____

_____

_____

TUESDAY_____/_____/_____

☐ sleep ☐ fatigue ☐ stress ☐ soreness

resting heart rate_____weight_____

planned workout_____

_____

_____

weather_____

route_____

_____

_____

dist._____time_____

zone 1_____2_____3_____4_____5_____

avg. HR_____avg. power_____

workout rating_____

notes _____

_____

_____

_____

_____

_____

_____

_____

nutrition _____

_____

_____

_____

week goals: ■ _____
■ _____
■ _____

WEDNESDAY ____/____/____

■ sleep ■ fatigue ■ stress ■ soreness

resting heart rate_____weight_____

planned workout_____

_____

_____

weather_____

route_____

_____

_____

_____

dist._____time_____

zone 1_____2_____3_____4_____5_____

avg. HR_____avg. power_____

workout rating_____

notes _____

_____

_____

_____

_____

_____

_____

_____

nutrition _____

_____

_____

_____

_____

THURSDAY ____/____/____

■ sleep ■ fatigue ■ stress ■ soreness

resting heart rate_____weight_____

planned workout_____

_____

_____

weather_____

route_____

_____

_____

_____

dist._____time_____

zone 1_____2_____3_____4_____5_____

avg. HR_____avg. power_____

workout rating_____

notes _____

_____

_____

_____

_____

_____

_____

_____

nutrition _____

_____

_____

_____

FRIDAY _____/_____/_____

☐ sleep ☐ fatigue ☐ stress ☐ soreness

resting heart rate_____weight_____

planned workout_____

_____

_____

weather_____

route_____

_____

_____

_____

_____

dist._____time_____

zone 1_____2_____3_____4_____5_____

avg. HR_____avg. power_____

workout rating_____

notes _____

_____

_____

_____

_____

_____

_____

_____

nutrition _____

_____

_____

_____

_____

SATURDAY _____/_____/_____

☐ sleep ☐ fatigue ☐ stress ☐ soreness

resting heart rate_____weight_____

planned workout_____

_____

_____

weather_____

route_____

_____

_____

_____

_____

_____

dist._____time_____

zone 1_____2_____3_____4_____5_____

avg. HR_____avg. power_____

workout rating_____

notes _____

_____

_____

_____

_____

_____

_____

_____

nutrition _____

_____

_____

_____

_____

SUNDAY _____/_____/_____

■ sleep ■ fatigue ■ stress ■ soreness

resting heart rate_____weight_____

planned workout_____

_____

_____

weather_____

route_____

_____

_____

_____

_____

dist._____time_____

zone 1_____2_____3_____4_____5_____

avg. HR_____avg. power_____

workout rating_____

notes _____

_____

_____

_____

_____

_____

_____

_____

_____

nutrition _____

_____

_____

_____

RACING

race 1 _____

category_____

distance_____time _____

result _____upgrade pts. _____

notes _____

_____

_____

_____

race 2 _____

category_____

distance_____time _____

result _____upgrade pts. _____

notes _____

_____

_____

WEEKLY SUMMARY

	weekly total	YTD
bike time		
bike miles		
strength time		
total		

soreness_____

notes _____

_____

_____

_____

_____

_____

Period: _____   **Planned Hours:** _____

MONDAY _____/_____/_____

▨ sleep ▨ fatigue ▨ stress ▨ soreness

resting heart rate_____weight_____

planned workout_____

_____

_____

weather_____

route_____

_____

_____

_____

dist._____time_____

zone 1_____2_____3_____4_____5_____

avg. HR_____avg. power_____

workout rating_____

notes _____

_____

_____

_____

_____

_____

_____

_____

nutrition _____

_____

_____

_____

_____

TUESDAY_____/_____/_____

▨ sleep ▨ fatigue ▨ stress ▨ soreness

resting heart rate_____weight_____

planned workout_____

_____

_____

weather_____

route_____

_____

_____

_____

dist._____time_____

zone 1_____2_____3_____4_____5_____

avg. HR_____avg. power_____

workout rating_____

notes _____

_____

_____

_____

_____

_____

_____

_____

nutrition _____

_____

_____

_____

_____

week goals: ■ _____
■ _____
■ _____

WEDNESDAY____/____/____

■ sleep ■ fatigue ■ stress ■ soreness

resting heart rate_____weight_____

planned workout_____

_____

_____

weather_____

route_____

_____

_____

_____

dist._____time_____

zone 1_____2_____3_____4_____5_____

avg. HR_____avg. power_____

workout rating_____

notes _____
_____
_____
_____
_____
_____
_____
_____
_____
_____

nutrition _____
_____
_____
_____
_____

THURSDAY____/____/____

■ sleep ■ fatigue ■ stress ■ soreness

resting heart rate_____weight_____

planned workout_____

_____

_____

weather_____

route_____

_____

_____

_____

dist._____time_____

zone 1_____2_____3_____4_____5_____

avg. HR_____avg. power_____

workout rating_____

notes _____
_____
_____
_____
_____
_____
_____
_____
_____
_____

nutrition _____
_____
_____
_____
_____

FRIDAY _____/_____/_____

- sleep - fatigue - stress - soreness

resting heart rate_____weight_____

planned workout_____

_____

_____

weather_____

route_____

_____

_____

_____

_____

dist._____time_____

zone 1_____2_____3_____4_____5_____

avg. HR_____avg. power_____

workout rating_____

notes _____

_____

_____

_____

_____

_____

_____

_____

nutrition _____

_____

_____

_____

_____

SATURDAY_____/_____/_____

- sleep - fatigue - stress - soreness

resting heart rate_____weight_____

planned workout_____

_____

weather_____

route_____

_____

_____

_____

_____

dist._____time_____

zone 1_____2_____3_____4_____5_____

avg. HR_____avg. power_____

workout rating_____

notes _____

_____

_____

_____

_____

_____

_____

_____

nutrition _____

_____

_____

_____

_____

SUNDAY _____/_____/_____

■ sleep ■ fatigue ■ stress ■ soreness

resting heart rate_____weight_____

planned workout_____

_____

_____

weather_____

route_____

_____

_____

_____

_____

dist._____time_____

zone 1_____2_____3_____4_____5_____

avg. HR_____avg. power_____

workout rating_____

notes _____

_____

_____

_____

_____

_____

_____

_____

_____

nutrition _____

_____

_____

_____

_____

RACING

race 1 _____

category_____

distance_____time _____

result _____upgrade pts._____

notes _____

_____

_____

_____

race 2 _____

category_____

distance_____time _____

result _____upgrade pts._____

notes _____

_____

_____

WEEKLY SUMMARY

	weekly total	YTD
bike time		
bike miles		
strength time		
total		

soreness _____

notes _____

_____

_____

_____

_____

_____

_____

week beginning:

Period: _____ **Planned Hours:** _____

MONDAY _____/_____/_____

■ sleep   ■ fatigue   ■ stress   ■ soreness

resting heart rate_____weight_____

planned workout_____

_____

_____

weather_____

route_____

_____

_____

_____

dist._____time_____

zone 1_____2_____3_____4_____5_____

avg. HR_____avg. power_____

workout rating_____

notes _____

_____

_____

_____

_____

_____

_____

_____

_____

_____

nutrition _____

_____

_____

_____

_____

TUESDAY_____/_____/_____

■ sleep   ■ fatigue   ■ stress   ■ soreness

resting heart rate_____weight_____

planned workout_____

_____

_____

weather_____

route_____

_____

_____

_____

dist._____time_____

zone 1_____2_____3_____4_____5_____

avg. HR_____avg. power_____

workout rating_____

notes _____

_____

_____

_____

_____

_____

_____

_____

_____

_____

nutrition _____

_____

_____

_____

_____

week goals: ◼ _____

◼ _____

◼ _____

WEDNESDAY___/___/___

◼ sleep ◼ fatigue ◼ stress ◼ soreness

resting heart rate_____weight_____

planned workout_____

_____

_____

weather_____

route_____

_____

_____

_____

dist._____time_____

zone 1_____2_____3_____4_____5_____

avg. HR_____avg. power_____

workout rating_____

notes _____

_____

_____

_____

_____

_____

_____

_____

_____

_____

nutrition _____

_____

_____

_____

_____

THURSDAY___/___/___

◼ sleep ◼ fatigue ◼ stress ◼ soreness

resting heart rate_____weight_____

planned workout_____

_____

weather_____

route_____

_____

_____

_____

dist._____time_____

zone 1_____2_____3_____4_____5_____

avg. HR_____avg. power_____

workout rating_____

notes _____

_____

_____

_____

_____

_____

_____

nutrition _____

_____

_____

_____

FRIDAY_____/_____/_____

◻ sleep ◻ fatigue ◻ stress ◻ soreness

resting heart rate_____weight_____

planned workout_____

_____

_____

weather_____

route_____

_____

_____

_____

_____

dist._____time_____

zone 1_____2_____3_____4_____5_____

avg. HR_____avg. power_____

workout rating_____

notes _____

_____

_____

_____

_____

_____

_____

_____

_____

nutrition _____

_____

_____

_____

_____

SATURDAY_____/_____/_____

◻ sleep ◻ fatigue ◻ stress ◻ soreness

resting heart rate_____weight_____

planned workout_____

_____

_____

weather_____

route_____

_____

_____

_____

_____

dist._____time_____

zone 1_____2_____3_____4_____5_____

avg. HR_____avg. power_____

workout rating_____

notes _____

_____

_____

_____

_____

_____

_____

_____

_____

nutrition _____

_____

_____

_____

_____

SUNDAY _____/_____/_____

■ sleep ■ fatigue ■ stress ■ soreness

resting heart rate_____weight_____

planned workout_____

_____

_____

weather_____

route_____

_____

_____

_____

_____

dist._____time_____

zone 1_____2_____3_____4_____5_____

avg. HR_____avg. power_____

workout rating_____

notes _____

_____

_____

_____

_____

_____

_____

_____

_____

_____

nutrition _____

_____

_____

_____

RACING

race 1 _____

category_____

distance_____time _____

result _____upgrade pts. _____

notes _____

_____

_____

_____

race 2 _____

category_____

distance_____time _____

result _____upgrade pts. _____

notes _____

_____

_____

_____

WEEKLY SUMMARY

	weekly total	YTD
bike time		
bike miles		
strength time		
total		

soreness _____

notes _____

_____

_____

_____

_____

_____

_____

_____

Period: _____   **Planned Hours:** _____

MONDAY _____/_____/_____

▢ sleep ▢ fatigue ▢ stress ▢ soreness

resting heart rate_____weight_____

planned workout_____

_____

_____

weather_____

route_____

_____

_____

_____

dist._____time_____

zone 1_____2_____3_____4_____5_____

avg. HR_____avg. power_____

workout rating_____

notes _____

_____

_____

_____

_____

_____

_____

_____

_____

_____

nutrition _____

_____

_____

_____

_____

TUESDAY_____/_____/_____

▢ sleep ▢ fatigue ▢ stress ▢ soreness

resting heart rate_____weight_____

planned workout_____

_____

_____

weather_____

route_____

_____

_____

_____

dist._____time_____

zone 1_____2_____3_____4_____5_____

avg. HR_____avg. power_____

workout rating_____

notes _____

_____

_____

_____

_____

_____

_____

_____

_____

_____

nutrition _____

_____

_____

_____

_____

week goals: ■ _____
■ _____
■ _____

WEDNESDAY___/___/___

■ sleep ■ fatigue ■ stress ■ soreness
resting heart rate_____weight_____
planned workout_____
_____
_____
weather_____
route_____
_____
_____
_____

dist._____time_____
zone 1_____2_____3_____4_____5_____
avg. HR_____avg. power_____
workout rating_____

THURSDAY____/____/____

■ sleep ■ fatigue ■ stress ■ soreness
resting heart rate_____weight_____
planned workout_____
_____
_____
weather_____
route_____
_____
_____
_____

dist._____time_____
zone 1_____2_____3_____4_____5_____
avg. HR_____avg. power_____
workout rating_____

notes _____
_____
_____
_____
_____
_____
_____
_____
_____
_____

nutrition _____
_____
_____
_____

notes _____
_____
_____
_____
_____
_____
_____
_____
_____
_____

nutrition _____
_____
_____
_____

FRIDAY_____/_____/_____

■ sleep ■ fatigue ■ stress ■ soreness

resting heart rate_____weight_____

planned workout_____

_____

_____

weather_____

route_____

_____

_____

_____

_____

dist._____time_____

zone 1_____2_____3_____4_____5_____

avg. HR_____avg. power_____

workout rating_____

notes _____

_____

_____

_____

_____

_____

_____

_____

_____

_____

nutrition _____

_____

_____

_____

_____

SATURDAY_____/_____/_____

■ sleep ■ fatigue ■ stress ■ soreness

resting heart rate_____weight_____

planned workout_____

_____

_____

weather_____

route_____

_____

_____

_____

_____

dist._____time_____

zone 1_____2_____3_____4_____5_____

avg. HR_____avg. power_____

workout rating_____

notes _____

_____

_____

_____

_____

_____

_____

_____

_____

nutrition _____

_____

_____

_____

SUNDAY _____/_____/_____

☐ sleep ☐ fatigue ☐ stress ☐ soreness

resting heart rate_____weight_____

planned workout_____

_____

_____

weather_____

route_____

_____

_____

_____

_____

dist._____time_____

zone 1_____2_____3_____4_____5_____

avg. HR_____avg. power_____

workout rating_____

notes _____

_____

_____

_____

_____

_____

_____

_____

_____

_____

nutrition _____

_____

_____

_____

RACING

race 1 _____

category_____

distance_____time _____

result _____upgrade pts. _____

notes _____

_____

_____

_____

race 2 _____

category_____

distance_____time _____

result _____upgrade pts. _____

notes _____

_____

_____

WEEKLY SUMMARY

	weekly total	YTD
bike time		
bike miles		
strength time		
total		

soreness _____

notes _____

_____

_____

_____

_____

_____

_____

week beginning:

Period: _____   **Planned Hours:** _____

MONDAY _____/_____/_____

■ sleep   ■ fatigue   ■ stress   ■ soreness

resting heart rate_____weight_____

planned workout_____

_____

_____

weather_____

route_____

_____

_____

dist._____time_____

zone 1_____2_____3_____4_____5_____

avg. HR_____avg. power_____

workout rating_____

notes _____

_____

_____

_____

_____

_____

_____

_____

_____

nutrition _____

_____

_____

_____

_____

TUESDAY _____/_____/_____

■ sleep   ■ fatigue   ■ stress   ■ soreness

resting heart rate_____weight_____

planned workout_____

_____

_____

weather_____

route_____

_____

_____

dist._____time_____

zone 1_____2_____3_____4_____5_____

avg. HR_____avg. power_____

workout rating_____

notes _____

_____

_____

_____

_____

_____

_____

_____

nutrition _____

_____

_____

_____

week goals: ■ _____
■ _____
■ _____

WEDNESDAY_____/_____/_____

■ sleep ■ fatigue ■ stress ■ soreness

resting heart rate_____weight_____

planned workout_____
_____
_____

weather_____

route_____
_____
_____
_____

dist._____time_____

zone 1_____2_____3_____4_____5_____

avg. HR_____avg. power_____

workout rating_____

notes _____
_____
_____
_____
_____
_____
_____
_____
_____

nutrition _____
_____
_____
_____

THURSDAY_____/_____/_____

■ sleep ■ fatigue ■ stress ■ soreness

resting heart rate_____weight_____

planned workout_____
_____
_____

weather_____

route_____
_____
_____
_____

dist._____time_____

zone 1_____2_____3_____4_____5_____

avg. HR_____avg. power_____

workout rating_____

notes _____
_____
_____
_____
_____
_____
_____
_____
_____

nutrition _____
_____
_____
_____

FRIDAY _____/_____/_____

■ sleep ■ fatigue ■ stress ■ soreness

resting heart rate_____weight_____

planned workout_____

_____

_____

weather_____

route_____

_____

_____

_____

_____

dist._____time_____

zone 1_____2_____3_____4_____5_____

avg. HR_____avg. power_____

workout rating_____

notes _____

_____

_____

_____

_____

_____

_____

_____

_____

nutrition _____

_____

_____

_____

_____

SATURDAY _____/_____/_____

■ sleep ■ fatigue ■ stress ■ soreness

resting heart rate_____weight_____

planned workout_____

_____

_____

weather_____

route_____

_____

_____

_____

_____

dist._____time_____

zone 1_____2_____3_____4_____5_____

avg. HR_____avg. power_____

workout rating_____

notes _____

_____

_____

_____

_____

_____

_____

_____

_____

nutrition _____

_____

_____

_____

_____

SUNDAY _____/_____/_____

☐ sleep ☐ fatigue ☐ stress ☐ soreness

resting heart rate_____weight_____

planned workout_____

_____

_____

weather_____

route_____

_____

_____

_____

_____

dist._____time_____

zone 1_____2_____3_____4_____5_____

avg. HR_____avg. power_____

workout rating_____

notes _____

_____

_____

_____

_____

_____

_____

_____

_____

nutrition _____

_____

_____

_____

_____

RACING

race 1 _____

category_____

distance_____time _____

result _____upgrade pts. _____

notes _____

_____

_____

_____

race 2 _____

category_____

distance_____time _____

result _____upgrade pts. _____

notes _____

_____

_____

WEEKLY SUMMARY

	weekly total	YTD
bike time		
bike miles		
strength time		
total		

soreness_____

notes _____

_____

_____

_____

_____

Period: _____

Planned Hours: _____

MONDAY _____/_____/_____

☐ sleep ☐ fatigue ☐ stress ☐ soreness

resting heart rate_____weight_____

planned workout_____

_____

_____

weather_____

route_____

_____

_____

_____

dist._____time_____

zone 1_____2_____3_____4_____5_____

avg. HR_____avg. power_____

workout rating_____

notes _____

_____

_____

_____

_____

_____

_____

_____

_____

nutrition _____

_____

_____

_____

_____

TUESDAY_____/_____/_____

☐ sleep ☐ fatigue ☐ stress ☐ soreness

resting heart rate_____weight_____

planned workout_____

_____

_____

weather_____

route_____

_____

_____

_____

dist._____time_____

zone 1_____2_____3_____4_____5_____

avg. HR_____avg. power_____

workout rating_____

notes _____

_____

_____

_____

_____

_____

_____

_____

_____

nutrition _____

_____

_____

_____

_____

week goals: ■ _____
■ _____
■ _____

WEDNESDAY___/___/___

■ sleep ■ fatigue ■ stress ■ soreness

resting heart rate_____weight_____

planned workout_____

_____

_____

weather_____

route_____

_____

_____

_____

dist._____time_____

zone 1_____2_____3_____4_____5_____

avg. HR_____avg. power_____

workout rating_____

notes _____

_____

_____

_____

_____

_____

_____

_____

_____

nutrition _____

_____

_____

_____

_____

THURSDAY___/___/___

■ sleep ■ fatigue ■ stress ■ soreness

resting heart rate_____weight_____

planned workout_____

_____

_____

weather_____

route_____

_____

_____

_____

dist._____time_____

zone 1_____2_____3_____4_____5_____

avg. HR_____avg. power_____

workout rating_____

notes _____

_____

_____

_____

_____

_____

_____

_____

_____

nutrition _____

_____

_____

_____

_____

FRIDAY _____/_____/_____

▢ sleep ▢ fatigue ▢ stress ▢ soreness

resting heart rate_____weight_____

planned workout_____

_____

_____

weather_____

route_____

_____

_____

_____

_____

dist._____time_____

zone 1_____2_____3_____4_____5_____

avg. HR_____avg. power_____

workout rating_____

notes _____

_____

_____

_____

_____

_____

_____

_____

_____

nutrition _____

_____

_____

_____

SATURDAY_____/_____/_____

▢ sleep ▢ fatigue ▢ stress ▢ soreness

resting heart rate_____weight_____

planned workout_____

_____

_____

weather_____

route_____

_____

_____

_____

_____

dist._____time_____

zone 1_____2_____3_____4_____5_____

avg. HR_____avg. power_____

workout rating_____

notes _____

_____

_____

_____

_____

_____

_____

_____

_____

nutrition _____

_____

_____

_____

SUNDAY _____/_____/_____

■ sleep ■ fatigue ■ stress ■ soreness

resting heart rate_____weight_____

planned workout_____

_____

_____

weather_____

route_____

_____

_____

_____

_____

dist._____time_____

zone 1_____2_____3_____4_____5_____

avg. HR_____avg. power_____

workout rating_____

notes _____

_____

_____

_____

_____

_____

_____

_____

_____

_____

nutrition _____

_____

_____

_____

RACING

race 1 _____

category _____

distance_____time _____

result _____upgrade pts. _____

notes _____

_____

_____

_____

race 2 _____

category _____

distance_____time _____

result _____upgrade pts. _____

notes _____

_____

_____

WEEKLY SUMMARY

	weekly total	YTD
bike time		
bike miles		
strength time		
total		

soreness_____

notes _____

_____

_____

_____

_____

_____

_____

Period: _____   **Planned Hours:** _____

MONDAY _____/_____/_____

☐ sleep ☐ fatigue ☐ stress ☐ soreness

resting heart rate_____weight_____

planned workout_____

_____

_____

weather_____

route_____

_____

_____

dist._____time_____

zone 1_____2_____3_____4_____5_____

avg. HR_____avg. power_____

workout rating_____

notes _____

_____

_____

_____

_____

_____

_____

_____

_____

nutrition _____

_____

_____

_____

TUESDAY_____/_____/_____

☐ sleep ☐ fatigue ☐ stress ☐ soreness

resting heart rate_____weight_____

planned workout_____

_____

_____

weather_____

route_____

_____

_____

dist._____time_____

zone 1_____2_____3_____4_____5_____

avg. HR_____avg. power_____

workout rating_____

notes _____

_____

_____

_____

_____

_____

_____

_____

_____

nutrition _____

_____

_____

_____

week goals: ■ _____
■ _____
■ _____

WEDNESDAY___/___/___

■ sleep ■ fatigue ■ stress ■ soreness

resting heart rate_____weight_____

planned workout_____

_____

_____

weather_____

route_____

_____

_____

_____

dist._____time_____

zone 1_____2_____3_____4_____5_____

avg. HR_____avg. power_____

workout rating_____

notes _____

_____

_____

_____

_____

_____

_____

_____

_____

_____

_____

nutrition _____

_____

_____

_____

THURSDAY_____/_____/_____

■ sleep ■ fatigue ■ stress ■ soreness

resting heart rate_____weight_____

planned workout_____

_____

_____

weather_____

route_____

_____

_____

_____

dist._____time_____

zone 1_____2_____3_____4_____5_____

avg. HR_____avg. power_____

workout rating_____

notes _____

_____

_____

_____

_____

_____

_____

_____

_____

_____

_____

nutrition _____

_____

_____

_____

FRIDAY _____/_____/_____

☐ sleep ☐ fatigue ☐ stress ☐ soreness

resting heart rate_____weight_____

planned workout_____

_____

_____

weather_____

route_____

_____

_____

_____

_____

dist._____time_____

zone 1_____2_____3_____4_____5_____

avg. HR_____avg. power_____

workout rating_____

notes _____

_____

_____

_____

_____

_____

_____

_____

_____

_____

nutrition _____

_____

_____

_____

_____

SATURDAY_____/_____/_____

☐ sleep ☐ fatigue ☐ stress ☐ soreness

resting heart rate_____weight_____

planned workout_____

_____

_____

weather_____

route_____

_____

_____

_____

_____

dist._____time_____

zone 1_____2_____3_____4_____5_____

avg. HR_____avg. power_____

workout rating_____

notes _____

_____

_____

_____

_____

_____

_____

_____

_____

_____

nutrition _____

_____

_____

_____

_____

SUNDAY _____/_____/_____

■ sleep ■ fatigue ■ stress ■ soreness

resting heart rate_____weight_____

planned workout_____

_____

_____

weather_____

route_____

_____

_____

_____

_____

dist._____time_____

zone 1_____2_____3_____4_____5_____

avg. HR_____avg. power_____

workout rating_____

notes _____

_____

_____

_____

_____

_____

_____

_____

_____

nutrition _____

_____

_____

_____

_____

RACING

race 1 _____

category_____

distance_____time_____

result _____upgrade pts. _____

notes _____

_____

_____

_____

race 2 _____

category_____

distance_____time_____

result _____upgrade pts. _____

notes _____

_____

_____

WEEKLY SUMMARY

	weekly total	YTD
bike time		
bike miles		
strength time		
total		

soreness _____

notes _____

_____

_____

_____

_____

_____

_____

Period: _____   **Planned Hours:** _____

MONDAY _____/_____/_____

☐ sleep ☐ fatigue ☐ stress ☐ soreness

resting heart rate_____weight_____

planned workout_____

_____

_____

weather_____

route_____

_____

_____

_____

dist._____time_____

zone 1_____2_____3_____4_____5_____

avg. HR_____avg. power_____

workout rating_____

notes _____

_____

_____

_____

_____

_____

_____

_____

nutrition _____

_____

_____

_____

_____

TUESDAY _____/_____/_____

☐ sleep ☐ fatigue ☐ stress ☐ soreness

resting heart rate_____weight_____

planned workout_____

_____

_____

weather_____

route_____

_____

_____

_____

dist._____time_____

zone 1_____2_____3_____4_____5_____

avg. HR_____avg. power_____

workout rating_____

notes _____

_____

_____

_____

_____

_____

_____

_____

nutrition _____

_____

_____

_____

_____

week goals: ■ _____
■ _____
■ _____

WEDNESDAY ____/____/____

■ sleep ■ fatigue ■ stress ■ soreness

resting heart rate_____weight_____

planned workout_____

_____

_____

weather_____

route_____

_____

_____

_____

dist._____time_____

zone 1_____2_____3_____4_____5_____

avg. HR_____avg. power_____

workout rating_____

notes _____

_____

_____

_____

_____

_____

_____

_____

_____

_____

nutrition _____

_____

_____

_____

_____

THURSDAY ____/____/____

■ sleep ■ fatigue ■ stress ■ soreness

resting heart rate_____weight_____

planned workout_____

_____

weather_____

route_____

_____

_____

_____

dist._____time_____

zone 1_____2_____3_____4_____5_____

avg. HR_____avg. power_____

workout rating_____

notes _____

_____

_____

_____

_____

_____

_____

_____

_____

nutrition _____

_____

_____

_____

_____

FRIDAY_____/_____/_____

☐ sleep ☐ fatigue ☐ stress ☐ soreness

resting heart rate_____weight_____

planned workout_____

_____

_____

weather_____

route_____

_____

_____

_____

dist._____time_____

zone 1_____2_____3_____4_____5_____

avg. HR_____avg. power_____

workout rating_____

notes _____
_____
_____
_____
_____
_____
_____
_____
_____

nutrition _____
_____
_____
_____
_____

SATURDAY_____/_____/_____

☐ sleep ☐ fatigue ☐ stress ☐ soreness

resting heart rate_____weight_____

planned workout_____

_____

_____

weather_____

route_____

_____

_____

_____

dist._____time_____

zone 1_____2_____3_____4_____5_____

avg. HR_____avg. power_____

workout rating_____

notes _____
_____
_____
_____
_____
_____
_____
_____
_____

nutrition _____
_____
_____
_____
_____

SUNDAY _____/_____/_____

■ sleep ■ fatigue ■ stress ■ soreness

resting heart rate_____weight_____

planned workout_____

_____

_____

weather_____

route_____

_____

_____

_____

_____

dist._____time_____

zone 1_____2_____3_____4_____5_____

avg. HR_____avg. power_____

workout rating_____

notes _____

_____

_____

_____

_____

_____

_____

_____

_____

_____

nutrition _____

_____

_____

_____

RACING

race 1 _____

category_____

distance_____time _____

result _____upgrade pts. _____

notes _____

_____

_____

_____

race 2 _____

category_____

distance_____time _____

result _____upgrade pts. _____

notes _____

_____

_____

_____

WEEKLY SUMMARY

	weekly total	YTD
bike time		
bike miles		
strength time		
total		

soreness_____

notes _____

_____

_____

_____

_____

_____

_____

Period: _____ **Planned Hours:** _____

MONDAY _____/_____/_____

■ sleep ■ fatigue ■ stress ■ soreness

resting heart rate_____weight_____

planned workout_____

_____

_____

weather_____

route_____

_____

_____

_____

dist._____time_____

zone 1_____2_____3_____4_____5_____

avg. HR_____avg. power_____

workout rating_____

notes _____

_____

_____

_____

_____

_____

_____

_____

_____

nutrition _____

_____

_____

_____

_____

TUESDAY_____/_____/_____

■ sleep ■ fatigue ■ stress ■ soreness

resting heart rate_____weight_____

planned workout_____

_____

_____

weather_____

route_____

_____

_____

_____

dist._____time_____

zone 1_____2_____3_____4_____5_____

avg. HR_____avg. power_____

workout rating_____

notes _____

_____

_____

_____

_____

_____

_____

_____

_____

nutrition _____

_____

_____

_____

_____

week goals: ▪ _____
▪ _____
▪ _____

WEDNESDAY____/____/____

▪ sleep ▪ fatigue ▪ stress ▪ soreness

resting heart rate_____weight_____

planned workout_____

_____

_____

weather_____

route_____

_____

_____

_____

dist._____time_____

zone 1____2____3____4____5____

avg. HR_____avg. power_____

workout rating_____

notes _____
_____
_____
_____
_____
_____
_____
_____
_____
_____
_____

nutrition _____
_____
_____
_____
_____

THURSDAY____/____/____

▪ sleep ▪ fatigue ▪ stress ▪ soreness

resting heart rate_____weight_____

planned workout_____

_____

_____

weather_____

route_____

_____

_____

_____

dist._____time_____

zone 1____2____3____4____5____

avg. HR_____avg. power_____

workout rating_____

notes _____
_____
_____
_____
_____
_____
_____
_____
_____
_____
_____

nutrition _____
_____
_____
_____
_____

FRIDAY _____/_____/_____

▪ sleep ▪ fatigue ▪ stress ▪ soreness

resting heart rate_____weight_____

planned workout_____

_____

_____

weather_____

route_____

_____

_____

_____

dist._____time_____

zone 1_____2_____3_____4_____5_____

avg. HR_____avg. power_____

workout rating_____

notes _____

_____

_____

_____

_____

_____

_____

_____

_____

nutrition _____

_____

_____

_____

SATURDAY _____/_____/_____

▪ sleep ▪ fatigue ▪ stress ▪ soreness

resting heart rate_____weight_____

planned workout_____

_____

_____

weather_____

route_____

_____

_____

_____

dist._____time_____

zone 1_____2_____3_____4_____5_____

avg. HR_____avg. power_____

workout rating_____

notes _____

_____

_____

_____

_____

_____

_____

_____

_____

nutrition _____

_____

_____

_____

_____

SUNDAY _____/_____/_____

■ sleep ■ fatigue ■ stress ■ soreness

resting heart rate_____weight_____

planned workout_____

_____

_____

weather_____

route_____

_____

_____

_____

dist._____time_____

zone 1_____2_____3_____4_____5_____

avg. HR_____avg. power_____

workout rating_____

_____

notes_____

_____

_____

_____

_____

_____

_____

_____

_____

_____

_____

nutrition _____

_____

_____

_____

RACING

race 1 _____

category_____

distance_____time _____

result _____upgrade pts. _____

notes _____

_____

_____

_____

race 2 _____

category_____

distance_____time _____

result _____upgrade pts. _____

notes _____

_____

_____

WEEKLY SUMMARY

	weekly total	YTD
bike time		
bike miles		
strength time		
total		

soreness _____

notes _____

_____

_____

_____

_____

_____

Period: _____   **Planned Hours:** _____

MONDAY _____/_____/_____

▇ sleep ▇ fatigue ▇ stress ▇ soreness

resting heart rate_____weight_____

planned workout_____

_____

_____

weather_____

route_____

_____

_____

_____

dist._____time_____

zone 1_____2_____3_____4_____5_____

avg. HR_____avg. power_____

workout rating_____

notes _____

_____

_____

_____

_____

_____

_____

_____

_____

nutrition _____

_____

_____

_____

_____

TUESDAY_____/_____/_____

▇ sleep ▇ fatigue ▇ stress ▇ soreness

resting heart rate_____weight_____

planned workout_____

_____

_____

weather_____

route_____

_____

_____

_____

dist._____time_____

zone 1_____2_____3_____4_____5_____

avg. HR_____avg. power_____

workout rating_____

notes _____

_____

_____

_____

_____

_____

_____

_____

_____

nutrition _____

_____

_____

_____

week goals: ■ _____
■ _____
■ _____

WEDNESDAY____/____/____

■ sleep ■ fatigue ■ stress ■ soreness

resting heart rate_____weight_____

planned workout_____

_____

_____

weather_____

route_____

_____

_____

_____

dist._____time_____

zone 1_____2_____3_____4_____5_____

avg. HR_____avg. power_____

workout rating_____

notes _____

_____

_____

_____

_____

_____

_____

_____

_____

_____

nutrition _____

_____

_____

_____

_____

THURSDAY____/____/____

■ sleep ■ fatigue ■ stress ■ soreness

resting heart rate_____weight_____

planned workout_____

_____

_____

weather_____

route_____

_____

_____

_____

dist._____time_____

zone 1_____2_____3_____4_____5_____

avg. HR_____avg. power_____

workout rating_____

notes _____

_____

_____

_____

_____

_____

_____

_____

_____

_____

nutrition _____

_____

_____

_____

_____

FRIDAY _____/_____/_____

■ sleep ■ fatigue ■ stress ■ soreness

resting heart rate_____weight_____

planned workout_____

_____

_____

weather_____

route_____

_____

_____

_____

dist._____time_____

zone 1_____2_____3_____4_____5_____

avg. HR_____avg. power_____

workout rating_____

notes _____

_____

_____

_____

_____

_____

_____

_____

_____

_____

nutrition _____

_____

_____

_____

_____

SATURDAY_____/_____/_____

■ sleep ■ fatigue ■ stress ■ soreness

resting heart rate_____weight_____

planned workout_____

_____

_____

weather_____

route_____

_____

_____

_____

dist._____time_____

zone 1_____2_____3_____4_____5_____

avg. HR_____avg. power_____

workout rating_____

notes _____

_____

_____

_____

_____

_____

_____

_____

_____

_____

nutrition _____

_____

_____

_____

_____

SUNDAY _____/_____/_____

■ sleep ■ fatigue ■ stress ■ soreness

resting heart rate_____weight_____

planned workout_____

_____

_____

weather_____

route_____

_____

_____

_____

dist._____time_____

zone 1_____2_____3_____4_____5_____

avg. HR_____avg. power_____

workout rating_____

notes _____

_____

_____

_____

_____

_____

_____

_____

_____

nutrition _____

_____

_____

_____

_____

RACING

race 1 _____

category_____

distance_____time _____

result _____upgrade pts. _____

notes _____

_____

_____

_____

race 2 _____

category_____

distance_____time _____

result _____upgrade pts. _____

notes _____

_____

_____

WEEKLY SUMMARY

	weekly total	YTD
bike time		
bike miles		
strength time		
total		

soreness _____

notes _____

_____

_____

_____

_____

_____

_____

_____

Period: _____   **Planned Hours:** _____

MONDAY _____/_____/_____

sleep ▪ fatigue ▪ stress ▪ soreness

resting heart rate_____weight_____

planned workout_____

_____

_____

weather_____

route_____

_____

_____

_____

dist._____time_____

zone 1_____2_____3_____4_____5_____

avg. HR_____avg. power_____

workout rating_____

notes _____

_____

_____

_____

_____

_____

_____

_____

_____

nutrition _____

_____

_____

_____

_____

TUESDAY_____/_____/_____

sleep ▪ fatigue ▪ stress ▪ soreness

resting heart rate_____weight_____

planned workout_____

_____

_____

weather_____

route_____

_____

_____

_____

dist._____time_____

zone 1_____2_____3_____4_____5_____

avg. HR_____avg. power_____

workout rating_____

notes _____

_____

_____

_____

_____

_____

_____

_____

_____

nutrition _____

_____

_____

_____

_____

week goals: ■ _____
■ _____
■ _____

WEDNESDAY ____/____/____

■ sleep ■ fatigue ■ stress ■ soreness

resting heart rate_____weight_____

planned workout_____

_____

_____

weather_____

route_____

_____

_____

_____

dist._____time_____

zone 1_____2_____3_____4_____5_____

avg. HR_____avg. power_____

workout rating_____

notes _____

_____

_____

_____

_____

_____

_____

_____

_____

_____

nutrition _____

_____

_____

_____

THURSDAY ____/____/____

■ sleep ■ fatigue ■ stress ■ soreness

resting heart rate_____weight_____

planned workout_____

_____

_____

weather_____

route_____

_____

_____

_____

dist._____time_____

zone 1_____2_____3_____4_____5_____

avg. HR_____avg. power_____

workout rating_____

notes _____

_____

_____

_____

_____

_____

_____

_____

_____

nutrition _____

_____

_____

_____

FRIDAY _____/_____/_____

▪ sleep ▪ fatigue ▪ stress ▪ soreness

resting heart rate_____weight_____

planned workout_____

_____

_____

weather_____

route_____

_____

_____

_____

dist._____time_____

zone 1_____2_____3_____4_____5_____

avg. HR_____avg. power_____

workout rating_____

notes _____

_____

_____

_____

_____

_____

_____

nutrition _____

_____

_____

_____

SATURDAY_____/_____/_____

▪ sleep ▪ fatigue ▪ stress ▪ soreness

resting heart rate_____weight_____

planned workout_____

_____

_____

weather_____

route_____

_____

_____

_____

dist._____time_____

zone 1_____2_____3_____4_____5_____

avg. HR_____avg. power_____

workout rating_____

notes _____

_____

_____

_____

_____

_____

_____

nutrition _____

_____

_____

_____

SUNDAY _____/_____/_____

■ sleep ■ fatigue ■ stress ■ soreness

resting heart rate_____weight_____

planned workout_____

_____

_____

weather_____

route_____

_____

_____

_____

_____

dist._____time_____

zone 1_____2_____3_____4_____5_____

avg. HR_____avg. power_____

workout rating_____

notes _____

_____

_____

_____

_____

_____

_____

_____

nutrition _____

_____

_____

_____

RACING

race 1 _____

category_____

distance_____time _____

result _____upgrade pts. _____

notes _____

_____

_____

_____

race 2 _____

category_____

distance_____time _____

result _____upgrade pts. _____

notes _____

_____

_____

WEEKLY SUMMARY

	weekly total	YTD
bike time		
bike miles		
strength time		
total		

soreness _____

notes _____

_____

_____

_____

_____

_____

_____

_____

week beginning:

Period: _____   **Planned Hours:** _____

MONDAY _____/_____/_____

■ sleep ■ fatigue ■ stress ■ soreness

resting heart rate_____weight_____

planned workout_____

_____

_____

weather_____

route_____

_____

_____

_____

dist._____time_____

zone 1_____2_____3_____4_____5_____

avg. HR_____avg. power_____

workout rating_____

notes _____

_____

_____

_____

_____

_____

_____

_____

_____

nutrition _____

_____

_____

_____

_____

TUESDAY_____/_____/_____

■ sleep ■ fatigue ■ stress ■ soreness

resting heart rate_____weight_____

planned workout_____

_____

_____

weather_____

route_____

_____

_____

_____

dist._____time_____

zone 1_____2_____3_____4_____5_____

avg. HR_____avg. power_____

workout rating_____

notes _____

_____

_____

_____

_____

_____

_____

_____

_____

nutrition _____

_____

_____

_____

_____

week goals: _____

■ _____

■ _____

WEDNESDAY____/____/____

■ sleep ■ fatigue ■ stress ■ soreness

resting heart rate_____weight_____

planned workout_____

_____

_____

weather_____

route_____

_____

_____

dist._____time_____

zone 1_____2_____3_____4_____5_____

avg. HR_____avg. power_____

workout rating_____

notes _____

_____

_____

_____

_____

_____

_____

_____

nutrition _____

_____

_____

_____

_____

THURSDAY_____/_____/_____

■ sleep ■ fatigue ■ stress ■ soreness

resting heart rate_____weight_____

planned workout_____

_____

_____

weather_____

route_____

_____

_____

dist._____time_____

zone 1_____2_____3_____4_____5_____

avg. HR_____avg. power_____

workout rating_____

notes _____

_____

_____

_____

_____

_____

_____

_____

nutrition _____

_____

_____

_____

_____

FRIDAY_____/_____/_____

■ sleep ■ fatigue ■ stress ■ soreness

resting heart rate_____weight_____

planned workout_____

_____

_____

weather_____

route_____

_____

_____

_____

_____

dist._____time_____

zone 1_____2_____3_____4_____5_____

avg. HR_____avg. power_____

workout rating_____

notes _____

_____

_____

_____

_____

_____

_____

_____

_____

_____

nutrition _____

_____

_____

_____

_____

SATURDAY_____/_____/_____

■ sleep ■ fatigue ■ stress ■ soreness

resting heart rate_____weight_____

planned workout_____

_____

_____

weather_____

route_____

_____

_____

_____

_____

dist._____time_____

zone 1_____2_____3_____4_____5_____

avg. HR_____avg. power_____

workout rating_____

notes _____

_____

_____

_____

_____

_____

_____

_____

_____

_____

nutrition _____

_____

_____

_____

SUNDAY _____/_____/_____

▢ sleep ▢ fatigue ▢ stress ▢ soreness

resting heart rate_____weight_____

planned workout_____

_____

_____

weather_____

route_____

_____

_____

_____

dist._____time_____

zone 1_____2_____3_____4_____5_____

avg. HR_____avg. power_____

workout rating_____

notes _____

_____

_____

_____

_____

_____

_____

_____

_____

nutrition _____

_____

_____

_____

_____

RACING

race 1 _____

category_____

distance_____time _____

result _____upgrade pts. _____

notes _____

_____

_____

_____

race 2 _____

category_____

distance_____time _____

result _____upgrade pts. _____

notes _____

_____

_____

WEEKLY SUMMARY

	weekly total	YTD
bike time		
bike miles		
strength time		
total		

soreness _____

notes _____

_____

_____

_____

_____

_____

_____

Period: _____

Planned Hours: _____

MONDAY _____/_____/_____

◼ sleep ◼ fatigue ◼ stress ◼ soreness

resting heart rate_____weight_____

planned workout_____

_____

_____

weather_____

route_____

_____

_____

_____

dist._____time_____

zone 1_____2_____3_____4_____5_____

avg. HR_____avg. power_____

workout rating_____

notes _____

_____

_____

_____

_____

_____

_____

_____

_____

nutrition _____

_____

_____

_____

_____

TUESDAY _____/_____/_____

◼ sleep ◼ fatigue ◼ stress ◼ soreness

resting heart rate_____weight_____

planned workout_____

_____

_____

weather_____

route_____

_____

_____

_____

dist._____time_____

zone 1_____2_____3_____4_____5_____

avg. HR_____avg. power_____

workout rating_____

notes _____

_____

_____

_____

_____

_____

_____

_____

_____

nutrition _____

_____

_____

_____

_____

week goals: ◼ _____
◼ _____
◼ _____

WEDNESDAY ____/____/____

◼ sleep ◼ fatigue ◼ stress ◼ soreness

resting heart rate_____weight_____

planned workout_____

_____

_____

weather_____

route_____

_____

_____

dist._____time_____

zone 1_____2_____3_____4_____5_____

avg. HR_____avg. power_____

workout rating_____

notes _____

_____

_____

_____

_____

_____

_____

_____

_____

nutrition _____

_____

_____

_____

_____

THURSDAY ____/____/____

◼ sleep ◼ fatigue ◼ stress ◼ soreness

resting heart rate_____weight_____

planned workout_____

_____

_____

weather_____

route_____

_____

_____

dist._____time_____

zone 1_____2_____3_____4_____5_____

avg. HR_____avg. power_____

workout rating_____

notes _____

_____

_____

_____

_____

_____

_____

_____

nutrition _____

_____

_____

_____

_____

FRIDAY _____/_____/_____

sleep ░ fatigue ░ stress ░ soreness

resting heart rate_____weight_____

planned workout_____

_____

_____

weather_____

route_____

_____

_____

_____

dist._____time_____

zone 1_____2_____3_____4_____5_____

avg. HR_____avg. power_____

workout rating_____

notes _____

_____

_____

_____

_____

_____

_____

_____

_____

_____

nutrition _____

_____

_____

_____

_____

SATURDAY _____/_____/_____

sleep ░ fatigue ░ stress ░ soreness

resting heart rate_____weight_____

planned workout_____

_____

_____

weather_____

route_____

_____

_____

_____

dist._____time_____

zone 1_____2_____3_____4_____5_____

avg. HR_____avg. power_____

workout rating_____

notes _____

_____

_____

_____

_____

_____

_____

_____

_____

_____

nutrition _____

_____

_____

_____

_____

SUNDAY _____ / _____ / _____

- sleep
- fatigue
- stress
- soreness

resting heart rate _____ weight _____

planned workout _____

_____

_____

weather _____

route _____

_____

_____

_____

_____

dist. _____ time _____

zone 1 _____ 2 _____ 3 _____ 4 _____ 5 _____

avg. HR _____ avg. power _____

workout rating _____

notes _____

_____

_____

_____

_____

_____

_____

_____

_____

_____

nutrition _____

_____

_____

_____

_____

RACING

race 1 _____

category _____

distance _____ time _____

result _____ upgrade pts. _____

notes _____

_____

_____

_____

race 2 _____

category _____

distance _____ time _____

result _____ upgrade pts. _____

notes _____

_____

_____

_____

WEEKLY SUMMARY

	weekly total	YTD
bike time		
bike miles		
strength time		
total		

soreness _____

notes _____

_____

_____

_____

_____

_____

_____

Period: _____ **Planned Hours:** _____

MONDAY _____/_____/_____

■ sleep ■ fatigue ■ stress ■ soreness

resting heart rate_____weight_____

planned workout_____

_____

_____

weather_____

route_____

_____

_____

dist._____time_____

zone 1_____2_____3_____4_____5_____

avg. HR_____avg. power_____

workout rating_____

notes _____

_____

_____

_____

_____

_____

_____

_____

nutrition _____

_____

_____

_____

_____

TUESDAY_____/_____/_____

■ sleep ■ fatigue ■ stress ■ soreness

resting heart rate_____weight_____

planned workout_____

_____

_____

weather_____

route_____

_____

_____

dist._____time_____

zone 1_____2_____3_____4_____5_____

avg. HR_____avg. power_____

workout rating_____

notes _____

_____

_____

_____

_____

_____

_____

_____

nutrition _____

_____

_____

_____

_____

week goals: ◼ _____

◼ _____

◼ _____

WEDNESDAY ____/____/____

◼ sleep ◼ fatigue ◼ stress ◼ soreness

resting heart rate_____weight_____

planned workout_____

_____

_____

weather_____

route_____

_____

_____

_____

dist._____time_____

zone 1_____2_____3_____4_____5_____

avg. HR_____avg. power_____

workout rating_____

notes _____

_____

_____

_____

_____

_____

_____

_____

_____

_____

nutrition _____

_____

_____

_____

_____

THURSDAY ____/____/____

◼ sleep ◼ fatigue ◼ stress ◼ soreness

resting heart rate_____weight_____

planned workout_____

_____

_____

weather_____

route_____

_____

_____

_____

dist._____time_____

zone 1_____2_____3_____4_____5_____

avg. HR_____avg. power_____

workout rating_____

notes _____

_____

_____

_____

_____

_____

_____

_____

_____

_____

nutrition _____

_____

_____

_____

_____

FRIDAY _____ / _____ / _____

☐ sleep ☐ fatigue ☐ stress ☐ soreness

resting heart rate_____weight_____

planned workout_____

_____

_____

weather_____

route_____

_____

_____

_____

_____

dist._____time_____

zone 1_____2_____3_____4_____5_____

avg. HR_____avg. power_____

workout rating_____

notes ## notes _____

_____

_____

_____

_____

_____

_____

_____

_____

_____

nutrition _____

_____

_____

_____

_____

SATURDAY _____ / _____ / _____

☐ sleep ☐ fatigue ☐ stress ☐ soreness

resting heart rate_____weight_____

planned workout_____

_____

_____

weather_____

route_____

_____

_____

_____

_____

dist._____time_____

zone 1_____2_____3_____4_____5_____

avg. HR_____avg. power_____

workout rating_____

notes _____

_____

_____

_____

_____

_____

_____

_____

_____

_____

nutrition _____

_____

_____

_____

_____

SUNDAY _____/_____/_____

■ sleep ■ fatigue ■ stress ■ soreness

resting heart rate_____weight_____

planned workout_____

_____

_____

weather_____

route_____

_____

_____

_____

dist._____time_____

zone 1_____2_____3_____4_____5_____

avg. HR_____avg. power_____

workout rating_____

notes _____

_____

_____

_____

_____

_____

_____

_____

_____

_____

nutrition _____

_____

_____

_____

RACING

race 1 _____

category_____

distance_____time _____

result _____upgrade pts._____

notes _____

_____

_____

_____

race 2 _____

category_____

distance_____time _____

result _____upgrade pts._____

notes _____

_____

_____

WEEKLY SUMMARY

	weekly total	YTD
bike time		
bike miles		
strength time		
total		

soreness _____

notes _____

_____

_____

_____

_____

_____

_____

Period: _____   **Planned Hours:** _____

MONDAY _____ / _____ / _____

☐ sleep ☐ fatigue ☐ stress ☐ soreness

resting heart rate_____weight_____

planned workout_____

_____

_____

weather_____

route_____

_____

_____

_____

dist._____time_____

zone 1_____2_____3_____4_____5_____

avg. HR_____avg. power_____

workout rating_____

notes _____

_____

_____

_____

_____

_____

_____

_____

_____

nutrition _____

_____

_____

_____

_____

TUESDAY _____ / _____ / _____

☐ sleep ☐ fatigue ☐ stress ☐ soreness

resting heart rate_____weight_____

planned workout_____

_____

_____

weather_____

route_____

_____

_____

_____

dist._____time_____

zone 1_____2_____3_____4_____5_____

avg. HR_____avg. power_____

workout rating_____

notes _____

_____

_____

_____

_____

_____

_____

_____

_____

nutrition _____

_____

_____

_____

week goals: ▪ _____
▪ _____
▪ _____

WEDNESDAY____/____/____

▪ sleep ▪ fatigue ▪ stress ▪ soreness

resting heart rate_____weight_____

planned workout_____

_____

_____

weather_____

route_____

_____

_____

_____

dist._____time_____

zone 1_____2_____3_____4_____5_____

avg. HR_____avg. power_____

workout rating_____

notes _____
_____
_____
_____
_____
_____
_____
_____
_____
_____

nutrition _____
_____
_____
_____
_____

THURSDAY_____/_____/_____

▪ sleep ▪ fatigue ▪ stress ▪ soreness

resting heart rate_____weight_____

planned workout_____

_____

_____

weather_____

route_____

_____

_____

_____

dist._____time_____

zone 1_____2_____3_____4_____5_____

avg. HR_____avg. power_____

workout rating_____

notes _____
_____
_____
_____
_____
_____
_____
_____
_____
_____

nutrition _____
_____
_____
_____
_____

FRIDAY _____/_____/_____

■ sleep　■ fatigue　■ stress　■ soreness

resting heart rate_____weight_____

planned workout_____

_____

_____

weather_____

route_____

_____

_____

_____

_____

dist._____time_____

zone 1_____2_____3_____4_____5_____

avg. HR_____avg. power_____

workout rating_____

notes _____

_____

_____

_____

_____

_____

_____

_____

_____

nutrition _____

_____

_____

_____

SATURDAY _____/_____/_____

■ sleep　■ fatigue　■ stress　■ soreness

resting heart rate_____weight_____

planned workout_____

_____

_____

weather_____

route_____

_____

_____

_____

_____

dist._____time_____

zone 1_____2_____3_____4_____5_____

avg. HR_____avg. power_____

workout rating_____

notes _____

_____

_____

_____

_____

_____

_____

_____

_____

nutrition _____

_____

_____

_____

SUNDAY _____/_____/_____

sleep ▢ fatigue ▢ stress ▢ soreness ▢

resting heart rate_____weight_____

planned workout_____

_____

_____

weather_____

route_____

_____

_____

_____

dist._____time_____

zone 1_____2_____3_____4_____5_____

avg. HR_____avg. power_____

workout rating_____

notes _____

_____

_____

_____

_____

_____

_____

_____

nutrition _____

_____

_____

_____

_____

RACING

race 1 _____

category_____

distance_____time _____

result _____upgrade pts. _____

notes _____

_____

_____

_____

race 2 _____

category_____

distance_____time _____

result _____upgrade pts. _____

notes _____

_____

_____

WEEKLY SUMMARY

	weekly total	YTD
bike time		
bike miles		
strength time		
total		

soreness _____

notes _____

_____

_____

_____

_____

_____

Period: _____   **Planned Hours:** _____

MONDAY _____/_____/_____

▪ sleep ▪ fatigue ▪ stress ▪ soreness

resting heart rate_____weight_____

planned workout_____

_____

_____

weather_____

route_____

_____

_____

_____

dist._____time_____

zone 1_____2_____3_____4_____5_____

avg. HR_____avg. power_____

workout rating_____

notes _____

_____

_____

_____

_____

_____

_____

_____

_____

nutrition _____

_____

_____

_____

_____

TUESDAY_____/_____/_____

▪ sleep ▪ fatigue ▪ stress ▪ soreness

resting heart rate_____weight_____

planned workout_____

_____

_____

weather_____

route_____

_____

_____

_____

dist._____time_____

zone 1_____2_____3_____4_____5_____

avg. HR_____avg. power_____

workout rating_____

notes _____

_____

_____

_____

_____

_____

_____

_____

_____

nutrition _____

_____

_____

_____

week goals: ▪ _____
▪ _____
▪ _____

WEDNESDAY ____/____/____   notes _____

▪ sleep ▪ fatigue ▪ stress ▪ soreness _____

resting heart rate_____weight_____ _____

planned workout_____ _____

_____ _____

_____ _____

weather_____ _____

route_____ _____

_____ _____

_____ _____

_____ _____

dist._____time_____ **nutrition** _____

zone 1_____2_____3_____4_____5_____ _____

avg. HR_____avg. power_____ _____

workout rating_____ _____

THURSDAY ____/____/____   notes _____

▪ sleep ▪ fatigue ▪ stress ▪ soreness _____

resting heart rate_____weight_____ _____

planned workout_____ _____

_____ _____

_____ _____

weather_____ _____

route_____ _____

_____ _____

_____ _____

_____ _____

dist._____time_____ **nutrition** _____

zone 1_____2_____3_____4_____5_____ _____

avg. HR_____avg. power_____ _____

workout rating_____ _____

FRIDAY_____/_____/_____

☐ sleep   ☐ fatigue   ☐ stress   ☐ soreness

resting heart rate_____weight_____

planned workout_____

_____

weather_____

route_____

_____

_____

_____

dist._____time_____

zone 1_____2_____3_____4_____5_____

avg. HR_____avg. power_____

workout rating_____

notes _____

_____

_____

_____

_____

_____

_____

nutrition _____

_____

_____

_____

_____

_____

SATURDAY_____/_____/_____

☐ sleep   ☐ fatigue   ☐ stress   ☐ soreness

resting heart rate_____weight_____

planned workout_____

_____

weather_____

route_____

_____

_____

_____

dist._____time_____

zone 1_____2_____3_____4_____5_____

avg. HR_____avg. power_____

workout rating_____

notes _____

_____

_____

_____

_____

_____

_____

nutrition _____

_____

_____

_____

_____

SUNDAY _____/_____/_____

■ sleep ■ fatigue ■ stress ■ soreness

resting heart rate_____weight_____

planned workout_____

_____

_____

weather_____

route_____

_____

_____

_____

_____

dist._____time_____

zone 1_____2_____3_____4_____5_____

avg. HR_____avg. power_____

workout rating_____

notes _____

_____

_____

_____

_____

_____

_____

_____

nutrition _____

_____

_____

_____

_____

_____

RACING

race 1 _____

category_____

distance_____time _____

result _____upgrade pts. _____

notes _____

_____

_____

_____

race 2 _____

category_____

distance_____time _____

result _____upgrade pts. _____

notes _____

_____

_____

WEEKLY SUMMARY

	weekly total	YTD
bike time		
bike miles		
strength time		
total		

soreness_____

notes _____

_____

_____

_____

_____

_____

_____

_____

Period: _____   **Planned Hours:** _____

MONDAY _____/_____/_____

☐ sleep ☐ fatigue ☐ stress ☐ soreness

resting heart rate_____weight_____

planned workout_____

_____

_____

weather_____

route_____

_____

_____

_____

dist._____time_____

zone 1_____2_____3_____4_____5_____

avg. HR_____avg. power_____

workout rating_____

notes _____

_____

_____

_____

_____

_____

_____

_____

_____

nutrition _____

_____

_____

_____

_____

_____

TUESDAY_____/_____/_____

☐ sleep ☐ fatigue ☐ stress ☐ soreness

resting heart rate_____weight_____

planned workout_____

_____

_____

weather_____

route_____

_____

_____

_____

dist._____time_____

zone 1_____2_____3_____4_____5_____

avg. HR_____avg. power_____

workout rating_____

notes _____

_____

_____

_____

_____

_____

_____

_____

_____

nutrition _____

_____

_____

_____

_____

week goals: ■ _____

■ _____

■ _____

_____

WEDNESDAY____/____/____

■ sleep ■ fatigue ■ stress ■ soreness

resting heart rate_____weight_____

planned workout_____

_____

_____

weather_____

route_____

_____

_____

_____

dist._____time_____

zone 1_____2_____3_____4_____5_____

avg. HR_____avg. power_____

workout rating_____

notes _____

_____

_____

_____

_____

_____

_____

_____

_____

_____

_____

_____

nutrition _____

_____

_____

_____

_____

THURSDAY_____/_____/_____

■ sleep ■ fatigue ■ stress ■ soreness

resting heart rate_____weight_____

planned workout_____

_____

_____

weather_____

route_____

_____

_____

_____

dist._____time_____

zone 1_____2_____3_____4_____5_____

avg. HR_____avg. power_____

workout rating_____

notes _____

_____

_____

_____

_____

_____

_____

_____

_____

nutrition _____

_____

_____

_____

FRIDAY _____/_____/_____

◻ sleep ◻ fatigue ◻ stress ◻ soreness

resting heart rate_____weight_____

planned workout_____

_____

_____

weather_____

route_____

_____

_____

_____

_____

dist._____time_____

zone 1_____2_____3_____4_____5_____

avg. HR_____avg. power_____

workout rating_____

notes _____

_____

_____

_____

_____

_____

_____

_____

_____

_____

nutrition _____

_____

_____

_____

_____

SATURDAY_____/_____/_____

◻ sleep ◻ fatigue ◻ stress ◻ soreness

resting heart rate_____weight_____

planned workout_____

_____

_____

weather_____

route_____

_____

_____

_____

dist._____time_____

zone 1_____2_____3_____4_____5_____

avg. HR_____avg. power_____

workout rating_____

notes _____

_____

_____

_____

_____

_____

_____

_____

_____

_____

nutrition _____

_____

_____

_____

_____

SUNDAY _____/_____/_____

☐ sleep ☐ fatigue ☐ stress ☐ soreness

resting heart rate_____weight_____

planned workout_____

_____

_____

weather_____

route_____

_____

_____

_____

dist._____time_____

zone 1_____2_____3_____4_____5_____

avg. HR_____avg. power_____

workout rating_____

notes _____

_____

_____

_____

_____

_____

_____

_____

_____

_____

_____

_____

nutrition _____

_____

_____

_____

_____

RACING

race 1 _____

category _____

distance_____time _____

result _____upgrade pts. _____

notes _____

_____

_____

_____

race 2 _____

category _____

distance_____time _____

result _____upgrade pts. _____

notes _____

_____

_____

WEEKLY SUMMARY

	weekly total	YTD
bike time		
bike miles		
strength time		
total		

soreness _____

notes _____

_____

_____

_____

_____

_____

_____

Period: _____   **Planned Hours:** _____

MONDAY _____/_____/_____

☐ sleep   ☐ fatigue   ☐ stress   ☐ soreness

resting heart rate_____weight_____

planned workout_____

_____

_____

weather_____

route_____

_____

_____

_____

dist._____time_____

zone 1_____2_____3_____4_____5_____

avg. HR_____avg. power_____

workout rating_____

notes _____

_____

_____

_____

_____

_____

_____

_____

_____

_____

_____

nutrition _____

_____

_____

_____

_____

TUESDAY_____/_____/_____

☐ sleep   ☐ fatigue   ☐ stress   ☐ soreness

resting heart rate_____weight_____

planned workout_____

_____

_____

weather_____

route_____

_____

_____

_____

dist._____time_____

zone 1_____2_____3_____4_____5_____

avg. HR_____avg. power_____

workout rating_____

notes _____

_____

_____

_____

_____

_____

_____

_____

_____

_____

_____

nutrition _____

_____

_____

_____

week goals: ■ _____
■ _____
■ _____

WEDNESDAY ____/____/____

■ sleep ■ fatigue ■ stress ■ soreness

resting heart rate_____weight_____

planned workout_____
_____
_____

weather_____

route_____
_____
_____
_____

dist._____time_____

zone 1_____2_____3_____4_____5_____

avg. HR_____avg. power_____

workout rating_____

notes _____
_____
_____
_____
_____
_____
_____
_____
_____

nutrition _____
_____
_____
_____
_____

THURSDAY ____/____/____

■ sleep ■ fatigue ■ stress ■ soreness

resting heart rate_____weight_____

planned workout_____
_____
_____

weather_____

route_____
_____
_____
_____

dist._____time_____

zone 1_____2_____3_____4_____5_____

avg. HR_____avg. power_____

workout rating_____

notes _____
_____
_____
_____
_____
_____
_____
_____
_____

nutrition _____
_____
_____
_____

FRIDAY _____/_____/_____

■ sleep ■ fatigue ■ stress ■ soreness

resting heart rate_____weight_____

planned workout_____

_____

_____

weather_____

route_____

_____

_____

_____

dist._____time_____

zone 1_____2_____3_____4_____5_____

avg. HR_____avg. power_____

workout rating_____

notes notes _____

_____

_____

_____

_____

_____

_____

_____

_____

nutrition _____

_____

_____

_____

_____

SATURDAY_____/_____/_____

■ sleep ■ fatigue ■ stress ■ soreness

resting heart rate_____weight_____

planned workout_____

_____

_____

weather_____

route_____

_____

_____

_____

dist._____time_____

zone 1_____2_____3_____4_____5_____

avg. HR_____avg. power_____

workout rating_____

notes _____

_____

_____

_____

_____

_____

_____

_____

_____

nutrition _____

_____

_____

_____

_____

SUNDAY ____ / ____ / ____

- sleep - fatigue - stress - soreness

resting heart rate_____weight_____

planned workout_____

_____

_____

weather_____

route_____

_____

_____

_____

dist._____time_____

zone 1_____2_____3_____4_____5_____

avg. HR_____avg. power_____

workout rating_____

notes _____

_____

_____

_____

_____

_____

_____

_____

_____

nutrition _____

_____

_____

_____

RACING

race 1 _____

category_____

distance_____time _____

result _____upgrade pts._____

notes _____

_____

_____

_____

race 2 _____

category_____

distance_____time _____

result _____upgrade pts._____

notes _____

_____

_____

WEEKLY SUMMARY

	weekly total	YTD
bike time		
bike miles		
strength time		
total		

soreness _____

notes _____

_____

_____

_____

_____

_____

_____

Period: _____   **Planned Hours:** _____

MONDAY _____/_____/_____   notes _____

■ sleep ■ fatigue ■ stress ■ soreness   _____

resting heart rate_____weight_____   _____

planned workout_____   _____

_____   _____

_____   _____

weather_____   _____

route_____   _____

_____   _____

_____   _____

_____   _____

dist._____time_____   **nutrition** _____

zone 1_____2_____3_____4_____5_____   _____

avg. HR_____avg. power_____   _____

workout rating_____   _____

TUESDAY_____/_____/_____   notes _____

■ sleep ■ fatigue ■ stress ■ soreness   _____

resting heart rate_____weight_____   _____

planned workout_____   _____

_____   _____

_____   _____

weather_____   _____

route_____   _____

_____   _____

_____   _____

_____   _____

dist._____time_____   **nutrition** _____

zone 1_____2_____3_____4_____5_____   _____

avg. HR_____avg. power_____   _____

workout rating_____   _____

week goals: ■ _____

■ _____

■ _____

WEDNESDAY___/___/___

■ sleep ■ fatigue ■ stress ■ soreness

resting heart rate_____weight_____

planned workout_____

_____

_____

weather_____

route_____

_____

_____

_____

dist._____time_____

zone 1_____2_____3_____4_____5_____

avg. HR_____avg. power_____

workout rating_____

_____

_____

_____

_____

_____

_____

_____

_____

_____

nutrition _____

_____

_____

_____

_____

THURSDAY___/___/___

■ sleep ■ fatigue ■ stress ■ soreness

resting heart rate_____weight_____

planned workout_____

_____

_____

weather_____

route_____

_____

_____

_____

dist._____time_____

zone 1_____2_____3_____4_____5_____

avg. HR_____avg. power_____

workout rating_____

notes _____

_____

_____

_____

_____

_____

_____

_____

_____

_____

nutrition _____

_____

_____

_____

_____

FRIDAY _____/_____/_____

■ sleep ■ fatigue ■ stress ■ soreness

resting heart rate_____weight_____

planned workout_____

_____

_____

weather_____

route_____

_____

_____

_____

_____

dist._____time_____

zone 1_____2_____3_____4_____5_____

avg. HR_____avg. power_____

workout rating_____

notes _____

_____

_____

_____

_____

_____

_____

_____

_____

nutrition _____

_____

_____

_____

_____

SATURDAY_____/_____/_____

■ sleep ■ fatigue ■ stress ■ soreness

resting heart rate_____weight_____

planned workout_____

_____

_____

weather_____

route_____

_____

_____

_____

_____

_____

dist._____time_____

zone 1_____2_____3_____4_____5_____

avg. HR_____avg. power_____

workout rating_____

notes _____

_____

_____

_____

_____

_____

_____

_____

_____

nutrition _____

_____

_____

_____

_____

SUNDAY _____/_____/_____

■ sleep ■ fatigue ■ stress ■ soreness

resting heart rate_____weight_____

planned workout_____

_____

_____

weather_____

route_____

_____

_____

_____

_____

dist._____time_____

zone 1_____2_____3_____4_____5_____

avg. HR_____avg. power_____

workout rating_____

notes _____

_____

_____

_____

_____

_____

_____

_____

_____

nutrition _____

_____

_____

_____

_____

RACING

race 1 _____

category_____

distance_____time _____

result _____upgrade pts. _____

notes _____

_____

_____

_____

race 2 _____

category_____

distance_____time _____

result _____upgrade pts. _____

notes _____

_____

_____

WEEKLY SUMMARY

	weekly total	YTD
bike time		
bike miles		
strength time		
total		

soreness _____

notes _____

_____

_____

_____

_____

_____

_____

Period: _____   **Planned Hours:** _____

MONDAY _____/_____/_____

☐ sleep ☐ fatigue ☐ stress ☐ soreness

resting heart rate_____weight_____

planned workout_____

_____

_____

weather_____

route_____

_____

_____

dist._____time_____

zone 1_____2_____3_____4_____5_____

avg. HR_____avg. power_____

workout rating_____

notes _____

_____

_____

_____

_____

_____

_____

_____

nutrition _____

_____

_____

_____

_____

TUESDAY_____/_____/_____

☐ sleep ☐ fatigue ☐ stress ☐ soreness

resting heart rate_____weight_____

planned workout_____

_____

_____

weather_____

route_____

_____

_____

dist._____time_____

zone 1_____2_____3_____4_____5_____

avg. HR_____avg. power_____

workout rating_____

notes _____

_____

_____

_____

_____

_____

_____

_____

nutrition _____

_____

_____

_____

_____

week goals: ■ _____
■ _____
■ _____

WEDNESDAY ____/____/____

■ sleep ■ fatigue ■ stress ■ soreness

resting heart rate_____weight_____

planned workout_____
_____
_____

weather_____

route_____
_____
_____
_____

dist._____time_____

zone 1_____2_____3_____4_____5_____

avg. HR_____avg. power_____

workout rating_____

notes _____
_____
_____
_____
_____
_____
_____
_____
_____

nutrition _____
_____
_____
_____
_____

THURSDAY ____/____/____

■ sleep ■ fatigue ■ stress ■ soreness

resting heart rate_____weight_____

planned workout_____
_____
_____

weather_____

route_____
_____
_____
_____

dist._____time_____

zone 1_____2_____3_____4_____5_____

avg. HR_____avg. power_____

workout rating_____

notes _____
_____
_____
_____
_____
_____
_____
_____
_____

nutrition _____
_____
_____
_____
_____

FRIDAY _____/_____/_____

☐ sleep ☐ fatigue ☐ stress ☐ soreness

resting heart rate_____weight_____

planned workout_____

_____

_____

weather_____

route_____

_____

_____

_____

_____

dist._____time_____

zone 1_____2_____3_____4_____5_____

avg. HR_____avg. power_____

workout rating_____

notes _____

_____

_____

_____

_____

_____

_____

_____

_____

_____

nutrition _____

_____

_____

_____

_____

SATURDAY _____/_____/_____

☐ sleep ☐ fatigue ☐ stress ☐ soreness

resting heart rate_____weight_____

planned workout_____

_____

_____

weather_____

route_____

_____

_____

_____

_____

dist._____time_____

zone 1_____2_____3_____4_____5_____

avg. HR_____avg. power_____

workout rating_____

notes _____

_____

_____

_____

_____

_____

_____

_____

_____

_____

nutrition _____

_____

_____

_____

_____

SUNDAY _____/_____/_____

□ sleep □ fatigue □ stress □ soreness

resting heart rate_____weight_____

planned workout_____

_____

weather_____

route_____

_____

_____

_____

dist._____time_____

zone 1_____2_____3_____4_____5_____

avg. HR_____avg. power_____

workout rating_____

notes _____

_____

_____

_____

_____

_____

_____

_____

_____

nutrition _____

_____

_____

_____

RACING

race 1 _____

category_____

distance_____time _____

result _____upgrade pts. _____

notes _____

_____

_____

_____

race 2 _____

category_____

distance_____time _____

result _____upgrade pts. _____

notes _____

_____

_____

WEEKLY SUMMARY

	weekly total	YTD
bike time		
bike miles		
strength time		
total		

soreness _____

notes _____

_____

_____

_____

_____

_____

Period: _____   **Planned Hours:** _____

MONDAY _____/_____/_____

☐ sleep ☐ fatigue ☐ stress ☐ soreness

resting heart rate_____weight_____

planned workout_____

_____

_____

weather_____

route_____

_____

_____

_____

dist._____time_____

zone 1_____2_____3_____4_____5_____

avg. HR_____avg. power_____

workout rating_____

notes _____

_____

_____

_____

_____

_____

_____

_____

_____

nutrition _____

_____

_____

_____

_____

TUESDAY_____/_____/_____

☐ sleep ☐ fatigue ☐ stress ☐ soreness

resting heart rate_____weight_____

planned workout_____

_____

_____

weather_____

route_____

_____

_____

_____

dist._____time_____

zone 1_____2_____3_____4_____5_____

avg. HR_____avg. power_____

workout rating_____

notes _____

_____

_____

_____

_____

_____

_____

_____

nutrition _____

_____

_____

_____

_____

week goals: ▪ _____

▪ _____

▪ _____

WEDNESDAY___/___/___

▪ sleep ▪ fatigue ▪ stress ▪ soreness

resting heart rate_____weight_____

planned workout_____

_____

_____

weather_____

route_____

_____

_____

_____

dist._____time_____

zone 1_____2_____3_____4_____5_____

avg. HR_____avg. power_____

workout rating_____

notes _____

_____

_____

_____

_____

_____

_____

_____

_____

nutrition _____

_____

_____

_____

_____

THURSDAY____/____/____

▪ sleep ▪ fatigue ▪ stress ▪ soreness

resting heart rate_____weight_____

planned workout_____

_____

_____

weather_____

route_____

_____

_____

_____

dist._____time_____

zone 1_____2_____3_____4_____5_____

avg. HR_____avg. power_____

workout rating_____

notes _____

_____

_____

_____

_____

_____

_____

_____

_____

nutrition _____

_____

_____

_____

_____

FRIDAY ____/____/____

▪ sleep ▪ fatigue ▪ stress ▪ soreness

resting heart rate_____weight_____

planned workout_____

_____

_____

weather_____

route_____

_____

_____

_____

dist._____time_____

zone 1_____2_____3_____4_____5_____

avg. HR_____avg. power_____

workout rating_____

notes _____

_____

_____

_____

_____

_____

_____

_____

_____

nutrition _____

_____

_____

_____

_____

SATURDAY ____/____/____

▪ sleep ▪ fatigue ▪ stress ▪ soreness

resting heart rate_____weight_____

planned workout_____

_____

_____

weather_____

route_____

_____

_____

_____

dist._____time_____

zone 1_____2_____3_____4_____5_____

avg. HR_____avg. power_____

workout rating_____

notes _____

_____

_____

_____

_____

_____

_____

_____

_____

nutrition _____

_____

_____

_____

_____

SUNDAY _____/_____/_____

■ sleep ■ fatigue ■ stress ■ soreness

resting heart rate_____weight_____

planned workout_____

_____

_____

weather_____

route_____

_____

_____

_____

_____

dist._____time_____

zone 1_____2_____3_____4_____5_____

avg. HR_____avg. power_____

workout rating_____

notes _____

_____

_____

_____

_____

_____

_____

_____

_____

_____

nutrition _____

_____

_____

_____

RACING

race 1 _____

category_____

distance_____time _____

result _____upgrade pts._____

notes _____

_____

_____

_____

race 2 _____

category_____

distance_____time _____

result _____upgrade pts._____

notes _____

_____

_____

WEEKLY SUMMARY

	weekly total	YTD
bike time		
bike miles		
strength time		
total		

soreness _____

notes _____

_____

_____

_____

_____

_____

_____

test results

DATE _____/_____/_____

test type _____

heart rate at AT _____

power at AT _____

	heart rate	power
zone 1	_____	_____
zone 2	_____	_____
zone 3	_____	_____
zone 4	_____	_____
zone 5a	_____	_____
zone 5b	_____	_____
zone 5c	_____	_____

VO_2 max _____% body fat _____

notes _____

_____

_____

DATE _____/_____/_____

test type _____

heart rate at AT _____

power at AT _____

	heart rate	power
zone 1	_____	_____
zone 2	_____	_____
zone 3	_____	_____
zone 4	_____	_____
zone 5a	_____	_____
zone 5b	_____	_____
zone 5c	_____	_____

VO_2 max _____% body fat _____

notes _____

_____

_____

DATE _____/_____/_____

test type _____

heart rate at AT _____

power at AT _____

	heart rate	power
zone 1	_____	_____
zone 2	_____	_____
zone 3	_____	_____
zone 4	_____	_____
zone 5a	_____	_____
zone 5b	_____	_____
zone 5c	_____	_____

VO_2 max _____% body fat _____

notes _____

_____

_____

DATE _____/_____/_____

test type _____

heart rate at AT _____

power at AT _____

	heart rate	power
zone 1	_____	_____
zone 2	_____	_____
zone 3	_____	_____
zone 4	_____	_____
zone 5a	_____	_____
zone 5b	_____	_____
zone 5c	_____	_____

VO_2 max _____% body fat _____

notes _____

_____

_____

DATE _____/_____/_____

test type_____

heart rate at AT_____

power at AT_____

	heart rate	**power**
zone 1	_____	_____
zone 2	_____	_____
zone 3	_____	_____
zone 4	_____	_____
zone 5a	_____	_____
zone 5b	_____	_____
zone 5c	_____	_____

VO_2 max _____% body fat _____

notes _____
_____
_____

DATE _____/_____/_____

test type_____

heart rate at AT_____

power at AT_____

	heart rate	**power**
zone 1	_____	_____
zone 2	_____	_____
zone 3	_____	_____
zone 4	_____	_____
zone 5a	_____	_____
zone 5b	_____	_____
zone 5c	_____	_____

VO_2 max _____% body fat _____

notes _____
_____
_____

DATE _____/_____/_____

test type_____

heart rate at AT_____

power at AT_____

	heart rate	**power**
zone 1	_____	_____
zone 2	_____	_____
zone 3	_____	_____
zone 4	_____	_____
zone 5a	_____	_____
zone 5b	_____	_____
zone 5c	_____	_____

VO_2 max _____% body fat _____

notes _____
_____
_____

DATE _____/_____/_____

test type_____

heart rate at AT_____

power at AT_____

	heart rate	**power**
zone 1	_____	_____
zone 2	_____	_____
zone 3	_____	_____
zone 4	_____	_____
zone 5a	_____	_____
zone 5b	_____	_____
zone 5c	_____	_____

VO_2 max _____% body fat _____

notes _____
_____
_____

training grids

When training information is graphed, trends are more easily seen. The grids provided on the next few pages could display weekly training hours or distances by sport; the longest weekly workout; the volume of weekly, race-specific intensity training (a good predictor of performance); or daily heart rates, either waking, recovery, or post-workout. You can probably come up with other creative ways to use this section. See pages 14 and 15 for more ideas on how to use the following grids.

month _____

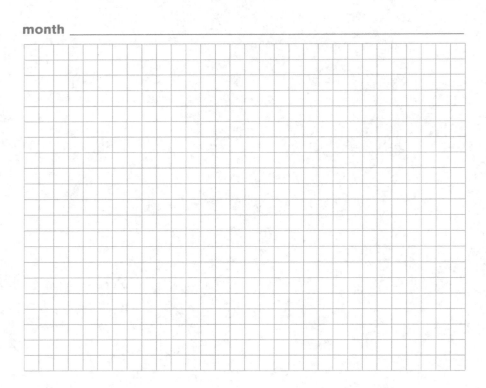

month _____

month _____

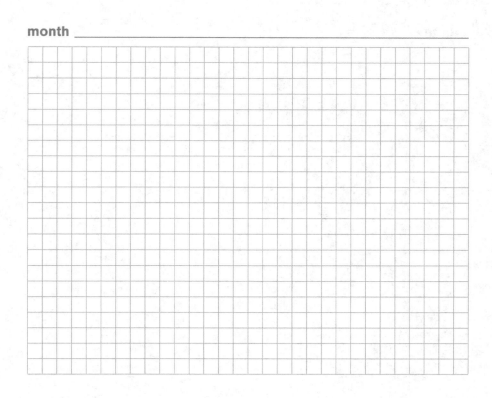

month _____

month _____

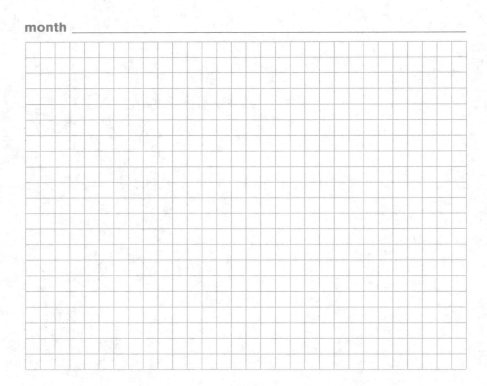

month _____

month _____

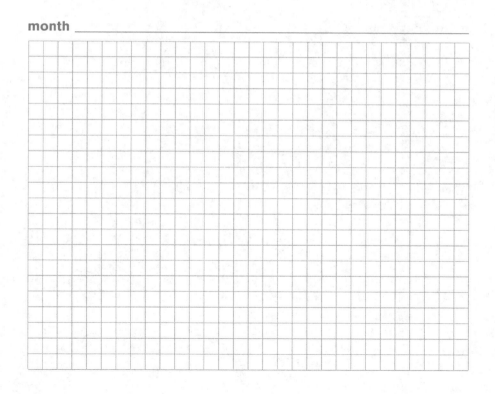

month _____

month _____

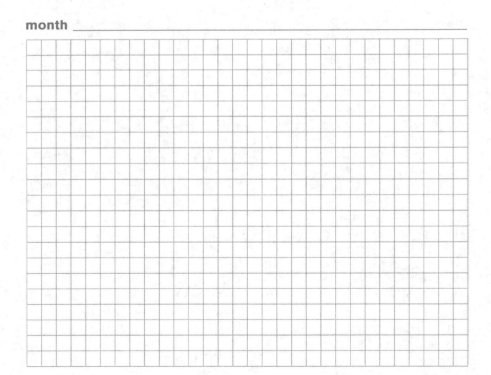

month _____

month _____

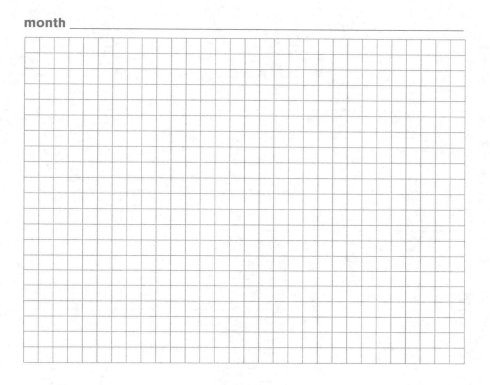

month _____

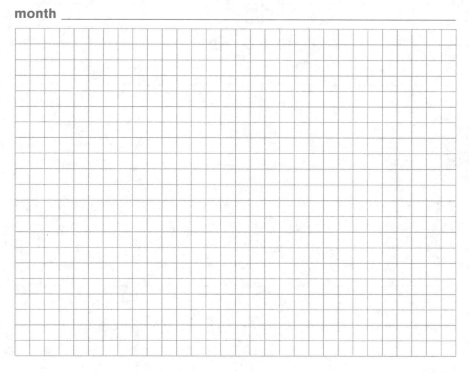

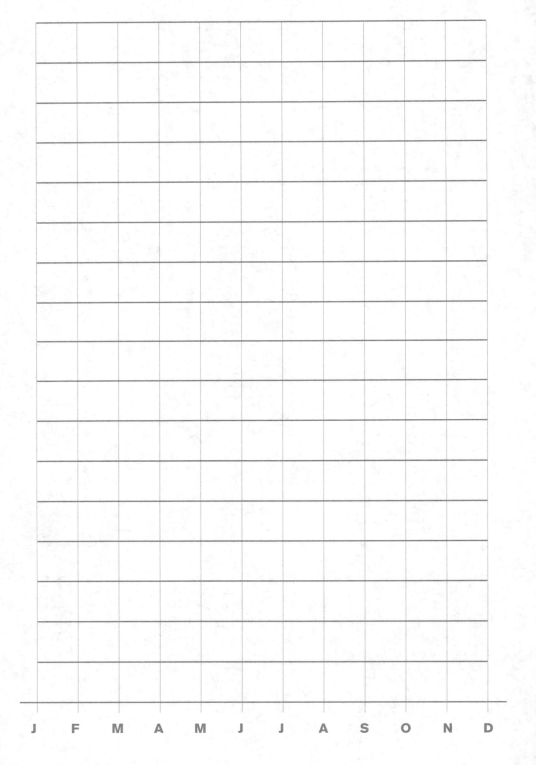

J F M A M J J A S O N D

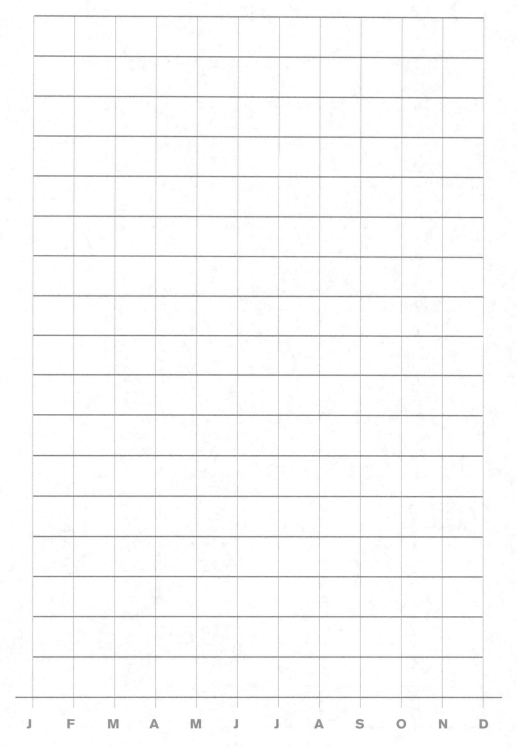

J F M A M J J A S O N D

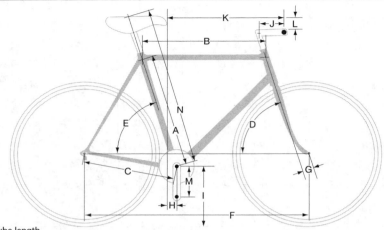

A. Seat tube length

B. Top tube length

C. Chainstay length

D. Head angle

E. Seat angle

F. Wheelbase

G. Fork offset

H. Seat setback

I. Bottom bracket height

J. Stem length

K. Reach

L. Seat-to-handlebar drop

M. Crank length

N. Seat height

Rear wheel spacing

Head tube diameter

Steering tube stack height

Seat tube diameter

Serial number

Date of purchase

■ *Seat height is measured from the center of the bottom bracket to the top of the saddle. The distance from the rails to the top of the saddle is not the same for all seats, so if you change saddles, this dimension may change.*

■ *Reach is measured from the nose of the saddle to the center of the bars. If you change saddles, remember that you may sit in a different position on the new saddle, and that may affect this dimension.*

■ *Crank length is measured from the center of the bottom bracket to the center of the pedal spindle.*

■ *Drop a weighted plumb line from the nose of the saddle to determine seat setback from the center of the bottom bracket.*

equipment changes

date	component	what was changed

mountain bike measurements

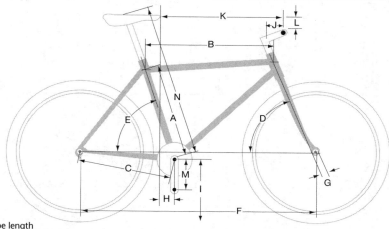

A. Seat tube length

B. Top tube length

C. Chainstay length

D. Head angle

E. Seat angle

F. Wheelbase

G. Fork offset

H. Seat setback

I. Bottom bracket height

J. Stem length

K. Reach

L. Seat-to-handlebar drop

M. Crank length

N. Seat height

Rear wheel spacing

Head tube diameter

Steering tube stack height

Seat tube diameter

Serial number

Date of purchase

■ *Seat height is measured from the center of the bottom bracket to the top of the saddle. The distance from the rails to the top of the saddle is not the same for all seats, so if you change saddles, this dimension may change.*

■ *Reach is measured from the nose of the saddle to the center of the bars. If you change saddles, remember that you may sit in a different position on the new saddle, and that may affect this dimension.*

■ *Crank length is measured from the center of the bottom bracket to the center of the pedal spindle.*

■ *Drop a weighted plumb line from the nose of the saddle to determine seat setback from the center of the bottom bracket.*

equipment changes

date	component	what was changed

routes and best times

route	date	time

season results

date	race	distance	place	comments

notes

race day
checklist

To reduce pre-race stress and the possibility of forgetting an important item of clothing or equipment, please use this checklist before leaving the house for your race. Better yet, use it the night before. You may not need everything, but you'll be sure to have it if the need arises.

- [ ] bike
- [ ] shoes
- [ ] helmet
- [ ] jersey
- [ ] shorts
- [ ] skinsuit
- [ ] socks
- [ ] tights/legwarmers
- [ ] jacket/armwarmers
- [ ] gloves
- [ ] sunglasses
- [ ] racing license
- [ ] racing number (if issued)
- [ ] safety pins

- [ ] course map/description
- [ ] vaseline
- [ ] water bottle
- [ ] water/energy drink
- [ ] food/energy bars
- [ ] pump
- [ ] tools
- [ ] lubricant
- [ ] spare cogs/wheels
- [ ] spare tube
- [ ] washcloth or towel
- [ ] rubbing alcohol
- [ ] cream/heat ointment
- [ ] first aid kit